CW00411657

The Girls Bathroom

Copyright © 2022 Sophia and Cinzia Limited

The right of The Girls' Bathroom to be identified as the Author of
the Work has been asserted by them in accordance with the
Copyright, Designs and Patents Act 1988.

First published in 2022 by
HEADLINE PUBLISHING GROUP

3

Apart from any use permitted under UK copyright law, this publication may
only be reproduced, stored, or transmitted, in any form, or by any means,
with prior permission in writing of the publishers or, in the case of reprographic
production, in accordance with the terms of licences issued by the Copyright
Licensing Agency.

Every effort has been made to fulfil requirements with regard to reproducing
copyright material. The author and publisher will be glad to rectify any omissions
at the earliest opportunity.

Cataloguing in Publication Data is available from the British Library

Hardback ISBN 978 1 4722 9276 6

Printed and bound in Italy by LEGO S.p.A

Designed by Nikki Ellis
Illustrations by Fabiola Gonzalez Betancourt
Cover design by Siobhan Hooper
Senior Commissioning Editor: Katie Packer
Copyeditor: Jill Cole
Proofreader: Helen Norris

Headline's policy is to use papers that are natural, renewable and recyclable
products and made from wood grown in well-managed forests and other
controlled sources. The logging and manufacturing processes are expected to
conform to the environmental regulations of the country of origin.

HEADLINE PUBLISHING GROUP
An Hachette UK Company
Carmelite House
50 Victoria Embankment
London EC4Y 0DZ

www.headline.co.uk
www.hachette.co.uk

FROM THE GIRLS BEHIND THE
CHART-TOPPING PODCAST

The Girls Bathroom

Living life messily and learning to love yourself

SOPHIA TUXFORD &
CINZIA BAYLIS-ZULLO

H

HEADLINE

For our listeners
and supporters,
thank you!

Contents

Introduction

Hey, guys. Oh my God, can you BELIEVE this? We have got a book out, what is going on?!!!!!

But hey, here we are, so . . . let's just jump in!

When we first started thinking about what we wanted to fill our book with, we kept coming back to the thousands of stories that you have shared with us, firstly on our YouTube channel and most recently on our podcast, *The Girls' Bathroom*. It's those stories that have allowed us to connect with so many of you on so many different levels, and those stories that have helped guide us all through the relationship dramas. We have honestly learnt so much from you and we know it's vice versa. This book is for anyone navigating the craziness of relationships, because from friendships to romance, professional networks and the most important relationship of all, the one you make with yourself, relationships are *everything*.

Our biggest hope is that this book will offer you a load of reassurance and help you to start resolving the overwhelming dilemmas that can literally floor you when you are going through them. Whatever you are dealing with, someone else out there has definitely been there, or is going through exactly the same kind of struggle right now, like, literally *this* second. On *The Girls' Bathroom*, where we address every single kind of relationship dilemma you can think of, the biggest hurdle is finding new, different issues to discuss, because many of the problems that our audience send to us are *so* similar. We receive hundreds and hundreds of emails and DMs, but perhaps our biggest discovery is how universal many of the challenges we face really are. We always say to each other, if only people knew how normal their situation was, that would bring them so much comfort.

In contrast to the 'girl squads' we're all meant to have from the beginning of school, what we've actually found is so many girls feel as if they've not got anyone to talk to about their problems in person. That was another one of the big reasons we wanted to write this book: to provide advice, empathy and support to anyone who is feeling lost or out of their depth and feel they have no one else to turn to. That's really where we try to help out a bit, to be the best friends that you might be missing in your life right now.

Before we go any further, unless you hadn't guessed, we are not doctors. We are not professionals; we do not actually know what we are talking about. This is a lighthearted space, so please don't take everything we say as gospel, because we could be wrong. And if there's anything serious that you are really struggling with, please contact a GP or a professional, because that is not us. We're just girls like you, trying to get through life.

It goes without saying that other people's problems are far easier to solve than your own. We have made so many mistakes along the way too! And as we've had the privilege of hearing your dilemmas for so many years, we really felt that it was now our turn to share a little more of our journeys, in case any of our stories could help you through bleak times.

Life is hard enough, so we wanted to make a book that you could dip in and out of if you're overwhelmed and for it to feel fun even when we talk about things that aren't perhaps the best times of our lives. We'd love for you to fold down corners and make notes in the notes sections, do the quizzes and highlight your favourite passages to come back to when there is something you perhaps need more reassurance on down the road. We absolutely don't want the book to feel mis in any way, even when we're talking about things that are sad – whether it's being pied off by a boy you like, or being excluded by your group of girlfriends. We all have shit times, believe us, we have *been there*. But we're eternal optimists and do believe that everything works out in the end. And whatever happens, you've got to laugh, haven't you?

Let's see how many problems we can solve and hurdles we can get over together.

Though we didn't realise it at the time, we started building our careers when we were barely sixteen. Back then, we were just obsessed with blogging and we could only dream and fantasise about what might be ahead for us. So many amazing, jaw-dropping things have happened to us over the past seven years, nearly all of them a hundred per cent positive. But of course, there have been some sticky moments to navigate too, and we were both really committed to not shying away from those in this book. This is not a PG version of what's happened, it's the actual version.

OK, time to crack on – let's see how many problems we can solve and hurdles we can get over together.

Sending you all our love, always

Sophia and *Cinzia*
xx

CHAPTER ONE

Telling Friends From Foes:

How Girlfriends Can Make or Break Your Happiness

While romantic relationships get all the attention in films and books, it's female friendships that are the bedrock, the anchor, the safe place that supports you through everything and whatever life throws at you. There for you through the bad times, celebrating with you through the good; while boyfriends might come and go, true friends are worth investing in. But that doesn't mean that finding and keeping your #girlsquad is easy – in fact, if your emails and messages are anything to go by, navigating girlfriendships is full of drama and heartache. One of the reasons we created our Girl Talk videos on YouTube and Girl Talk dilemmas on the podcast was that we were being inundated with requests for advice on female friendships from our audience. Because we are fortunate enough to have such a solid, healthy friendship, we are often asked about how we would cope with certain situations, some of which can be incredibly hurtful.

From reflecting on everything we have learnt, it's clear that it's basically impossible to get through school, uni, work and your social life unscathed by girl-group politics. While it may not seem like it from everyone's photos on Instagram, struggles with toxic friends, betrayal, feelings that your lives have fallen out of sync, and jealousy are all so typical, they're textbook. While we do believe it is important to learn to identify some of the more negative behaviours common to girl groups, we always prefer to focus on what the 'good' looks like and help empower you to find friends who help make you the best version of yourself day in and day out.

We want to share some of our formative experiences with forging friendships as well as talking through some of the most frequent themes we get asked for advice about. We absolutely believe that when it comes to girlfriendships, there are no devils or angels and most often hurtful situations usually occur because there are more issues going on than first meet the eye. Has your friend who is leaving you out become jealous of your relationship with someone else? Does she feel left behind because of your new life with your boyfriend? Try to scratch the surface to get to the real issue. While there is never any excuse for bullying or abuse, a lot of toxic behaviour stems from painful experiences from the past, and healthy relationships do not come naturally to lots and lots of people. That doesn't mean you can't grow and relearn some of your behaviours to become a better friend, but you do have to look in the mirror and remember that relationships are a two-way street. We always question ourselves and try to reflect on our own side first before making any decisions.

We really hope this will help to put any of your struggles or dilemmas with girlfriendships in context and give you some pointers on how you can help steer beyond any conflicts. Oh my God, we know it's not easy to keep your head held high when all you want to do is cry in your pillow every morning. But keeping a bit of perspective and remembering that there are amazing women out there, amazing friends whom you might not have even met yet, can help to keep you focused on the positive, no matter how difficult the problems you are going through with your friends. Sometimes, as sad as it might seem, you do just have to close that door to open the one that is waiting for you.

Dilemma One

I'm really struggling in my group of friends at school. I feel like I'm on the outside of everything and that my friends all like each other more than me. What should I do?

S: While Cinzia and I had each other, we were also part of a big girl group at school up to sixth form. When you're young, you have absolutely no perspective or experience of relationships to be able to judge what is OK and what's not. School is the beginning and the end of your world. It's your entire universe. Because your life is centred around school, both physically and psychologically, and it's all you've ever known, it's really hard to comprehend that soon you're actually not going to be there every day. That you may not have any association whatsoever with your school friends. If you could just think, *Well, fuck it, I'll do what I want*, none of the rubbish that goes on between you and other people in your school would matter.

C: I wish we'd had a Sophia and Cinzia to tell us that school wasn't going to matter to us one day in the very near future. Obviously, our families said that, but you don't listen to them, do you? Of course, school is important, to an extent – especially if you need to get specific grades to follow your own dreams. But it is just not *everything* in the way you think it is. When you're in it, it feels impossible to step outside, because you think, *Well, what is life without school and the people that go there?*

S: We did have some really good times with our group of friends, but girl issues are part and parcel of the school experience. If you get through school without having been caught up in the dynamics of girl-group politics at some point, you're basically a unicorn, because it feels like it's impossible not to get sucked in somehow. So many girls feel like it's only them suffering from these kinds of problems, and most people don't want to admit how hard it can be. But honestly, nearly all of us have been there.

There were definitely some learnings that we have taken away and still refer back to, to this day. For example, sometimes a friend would be really good fun and you'd think, *Aw, she's great really*. But other days, there could be cattiness or a real lack of tact. It might be constant little digs about your clothes or how you looked. It could be being laughed at (rather than with) and people trying to make you feel small about your ideas and dreams. It's always hard to know what to do, or what to say back, in these situations. But that walking-on-eggshells feeling of unpredictability with a friend – will she be nice today or not? – is the kind of behaviour that should set alarm bells ringing.

C: Another red flag is when a friend speaks very poorly about others, but becomes incredibly friendly to them in person. In that instance, you can pretty much guarantee she is doing the exact same thing to you, behind your back. We always encourage women to lift each other up. Obviously (!) we are only human and sometimes even the best of friends can get on your nerves. But I cannot think of a time that I have said anything about Sophia that I wouldn't say to her face. Even now, I'm scraping the barrel to even imagine what it would be about.

S: I think a big warning sign is a friend who never celebrates your wins, but instead takes the piss in front of other people about things that bring you joy. If this happens repeatedly, you just know they are not there for you. It can be hard to admit it to yourself, but it's true. If it feels like a friend never wants you to succeed, or at least not to succeed beyond her, in any avenue of life, and belittles you until you feel like you're locked in an exhausting game of one-upmanship that she always had to win, it's fair to say, this friend does not deserve her place on your train.

Making you feel left out is definitely a way that a friend or friends can make you feel disempowered and at least temporarily make themselves feel bigger, which is toxic behaviour. By leaning into their bond, while leaving you out, they will feel more secure. But it's never OK if a friend makes you feel like Billy No-Mates, especially if you don't feel you can broach the subject with her. Our advice would always be to invest your precious energy elsewhere. And if she suddenly starts to pay you attention when she realises you are forming other relationships, you know it was always about her issues with security rather than anything you did or didn't do.

C: When you are in a school, or uni, or office environment, when you have to see people on a regular basis, it's so easy to let these friendships drag on simply because you don't want to fall out – or even worse, get on your friends' wrong side. When you're young, you just can't see the true motivations behind the way people behave, you just haven't had enough experience to see it coming. I never once thought, maybe they're being unkind because they feel insecure about something. Perhaps she's trying to sabotage that girl's friendship or trying to make this one feel embarrassed about what she's wearing or doing, because it makes her feel bad about herself. As we've got older and learnt from our community about their experiences, we've realised jealousy is very often at the heart of a lot of this behaviour and if your friend isn't in a position to work on those underlying issues, the problems aren't going away. The only way you can protect yourself is to create distance and build your life in a direction away from the negativity.

Dilemma Two

All my friends seem to know what they want to do and are making plans to do it together, but I want to go down a different path after school. A big part of me is scared that if I do decide to go my own way, I'll lose all my friends and they'll laugh at me. I'm not even sure if I'll be any good at what I really want to do.

C: Soph and I always knew we wanted to go down a different route from the rest of our friends. They were all focused on going to uni and going on to study and do all those amazing things, which was just not what Sophia and I saw for ourselves. Though to be fair, we weren't that clear on what that was going to look like. I thought we might want to work for ourselves and that it might be something related to fashion, but it was very vague.

S: Even though we found A-levels a massive slog, we always worked really hard at school. Like, we were proper hard-working students. It was just unfortunate that we weren't very academic. We did try, though. We would always have our homework in on time, we'd be up late revising, and I remember Cinz carrying around these pages and pages of notes. We definitely weren't like those people who just didn't bother at all. We wanted to get good grades *so* badly, because at the time we'd been told that our life was over if we didn't. Spoiler alert: this was not accurate. But at the time, we thought our very futures depended on the grades.

C: Anyway, it was all hell really, because we were being pushed into something that we were a) not interested in, and b) not very good at either. So, we came to the conclusion that we needed something in our lives that we were both interested in and good at, and that's where the idea for the blog came in. We definitely dreamt of becoming fashion bloggers, alongside the magazines and shops that we were opening – but *all* of it felt like a total fantasy at the time. And like you, we were really nervous to tell our friends we were doing something different, because we were scared they wouldn't support it.

S: Whenever you try something different at school and beyond, there are going to be people who have something not exactly positive to say about it, but that doesn't mean you shouldn't do it. As the quote goes, 'If you live for the praise of people, you will die from their criticism', and I wish someone would have told me that more when I was younger. At school, that criticism can fill you with deep dread. Because we were so nervous about publishing our blog, we called it 'The Lifestyle Blog'. Really, we had wanted to call it 'Sophia & Cinzia', but then we thought, *Oh God, people are going to find it and give us a hard time about it.*

C: We worked really hard on that name. It took us a long time.

S: It's the shittiest name, isn't it? Looking back, goodness me. But there it was, 'The Lifestyle Blog'. From the moment we set it up, we also had a corresponding Instagram account, which we launched to absolutely zero fanfare on the exact same day. We were really excited and thought that we'd been really smart about disguising the whole thing.

C: Sadly, our covert operations didn't quite come off as we'd hoped. Somehow, everyone found out about it all on day *one*. I still don't know how. But literally the day after we set it live, a link was posted in our friendship group's WhatsApp chat, and our hearts sank through the floor. I thought it was the end of the world at the time. There was no, 'Girls, this is amazing, let's all follow it!' In fact, no one followed it.

S: Cinz was like, 'I need to rethink my education from this point.' She kept banging on about home-schooling.

C: But after a while, everything simmered down. We stayed really dedicated to the blog and we posted religiously every week. It was obviously a little quiet at the start – you know, just Soph and I refreshing the page. And maybe our nans looking at it. Pretty much no one else. Soon we decided to launch a YouTube channel to support it, because we both felt if we could film our outfits, instead of just taking pictures, it could help get our personality across a bit more.

S: We decided that we weren't going to speak in the videos, to make it as inoffensive as possible. It's so sad that we felt like we had to limit ourselves and what we did because of what other people were going to say about it, but if you've been in that kind of environment, you'll know how hard it is to step outside of other people's judgements.

Build your life in a direction away from negativity.

C: One day, the week after we started YouTube, we were in the cafeteria and someone shouted, 'Like and Subscribe!' and it felt like the whole room burst into laughter, with us the butt of the joke. I remember Soph saying, 'Pretend you didn't hear, pretend you didn't hear.'

S: Because there were two of us and we were in it together, nothing felt so bad, but very soon our group of friends had started to distance themselves from us and it really did crush us at the time. I feel so deeply for those people who go through this kind of thing alone, it can be so painful and ostracising. It's an experience so many of our community have been through and we want to say to you now: if a friend doesn't support your dreams, they aren't a friend. There are so many people in the world who will embrace you and love you for who you are and what you want to become one day.

   After this all happened, we realised that the rest of the group had decided not to sit with us at lunch, and because it was so obvious that we had been edged out, we started eating our lunches in my car.

C: It was sad, and the transition wasn't easy, but ultimately true friends would never treat you in this way and it made me value my friendship with Sophia all the more. There are always people out there who will support you and back you and celebrate your differences, and we all deserve to find those people. Just like when it comes to men, you don't ever have to settle.

S: When we're young, we can all be incredibly impressionable and find it easy to go along with the majority at school. So stepping outside of that can be a big leap when it's not the 'norm'. But sitting here now aged twenty-three do we wish we had done anything different?

C: Absolutely not. Follow your dreams, not someone else's. The right people will come with you on that journey.

Dilemma Three

I'm just about to turn twenty and I don't really have a group of friends. I have a handful of good girls in my life, but they don't know each other and they are all really different, so I can't ever imagine them becoming close. I feel really lonely when I think about it.

C: We get this kind of dilemma so, so, so often.

S: It's like we've been conditioned to think we have to have this interconnected girl gang.

C: When I read this, all I think is how lucky you are to have a handful of good girls.

S: Right?

C: But we get it. The idea of the girl group is so powerful and if you don't have one, it's easy to wonder if there's something missing. For us, after our experiences, we realised that we aren't suited to being in a girl group, and since school we've never formed another one. Of course, we've got close friends besides each other, but I think when you reach adulthood, individual friendships rather than interconnected groups are the reality for most people. As you mature, you all have your own lives, and it's not like school where you have to run with a crowd or you're an outsider. Adult female friendships can deal with space and time passing. We have friends with kids, and friends who are married or living in different places, and when you are with them it's wonderful and you connect, but months might pass in between, because everyone has so much going on.

S: Now it would feel unnatural for us to be in a situation where we were in constant communication on a daily basis with a group of eight or more girls. As Cinz and I work together, it's a bit different, but that deep need for a squad of girls around you just becomes so quickly obsolete – no matter what you might see on Instagram. We always say on the podcast that you *don't* need a group of friends. The truth is that you are going to meet different people throughout your life, and those people will come and go and add their contribution, then a door might close. And importantly, all those amazing friends might not be friends with each other.

Follow your dreams, not someone else's.

C: When you feel concerned you don't have 'enough' friends or that you aren't seeing friends enough, remember everything in pictures always looks better than it seems. The highlight reel of friendships people post is nothing like the reality; they could be having disagreements, they might be feeling distant, they could even be lonely. And all these things are normal and OK! From our own experiences, and the thousands of experiences that have been through the podcast, we know friendship isn't a one-size-fits-all concept, and that you have to find something that works for you and uplifts you as well as find people whom you genuinely want to see, uplift and love back.

S: Big friendship groups that are loving and supportive are a very rare breed. I absolutely would have loved to have stayed part of a super-close group that grew together and managed to navigate different experiences, but the likelihood of that is so low. Not all personalities match, and it's hard to bind so many individuals, all with competing aspirations and motivations, into one harmonious crowd and have them all connect with each other and gel through life's milestones. If it were that easy, everyone in the world would be friends. You just can't sync up with everyone, or even the majority of people. And nor should you feel any pressure to do so, because that is when you can get caught up in the toxic tangle, and *no one* wants that.

Dilemma Four

What should you look for in a best friend? How did you two know that your friendship was going to be so positive?

C: Sophia and I met in ballet class in the local church hall, just outside Nottingham, aged five, so the story of our lives before each other is very short. As a little girl and the eldest of three sisters, all I dreamt of being was a ballerina and ballet would always be mine and Soph's special place, all the way through to when we were sixteen. We have always had so many things in common, even back then.

S: While we were in the same school class from four through to eighteen, our friendship was truly built outside of the school gates, and that bond was special in ways that we didn't appreciate until we grew up a bit. Three times a week, for two hours, up until we were sixteen, we danced – it was a huge part of our young lives and something that was just for us.

C: It wasn't like we were exactly the same though. Soph was much more of a tomboy and we weren't *best friends* for a good long while. But things changed between us when we started secondary school, and we became closer and closer until we got to Year 8, when we were clearly besties. Even as thirteen-year-olds, we'd spend our lunchtimes plotting what we were going to do when we grew up. It would be, why don't we have our own shop? And we'd pore over a piece of paper, drawing out the shopfront, or spend hours coming up with our logo. Or we'd create our own magazine and then spend days planning what we'd call it. We'd then go home and create the front cover in Word on Soph's computer, and get so excited dreaming about what it would be like. We always had huge dreams and were into the idea of doing something creative with our lives.

As we've grown, I've realised that we do share a lot of things in our personalities and the way we form relationships. Neither Sophia nor I are confrontational. The last thing I'd do is have a fight or a screaming match with someone. We are both pretty chill and that has been the case throughout our friendship. While I don't think you necessarily need to have the same interests or aspirations, I do think that things can get tricky when you have very different energy.

Going through that difficult last year of school together also brought Soph and me closer. It was tough at times, and we had to really dig deep. We would constantly tell each other that we were going to do great things, to help prop each other up, and I think that really helped us articulate what we wanted for the future. It also formed the basis of the way in which we have manifested our current lives, something special, which we will explore later in this book.

S: Often you don't know how relationships will fare until they are tested, so there is no tried and true way of working out if someone is going to be important to you before you invest time in getting to know them. That can be a really intimidating thing, but our advice would always be not to look for a 'best friend', instead just try to get to know people who you share a connection with and take it from there.

Nine textbook toxic tells

1 THEY NEVER CELEBRATE YOUR WINS.

Does your friend seem to struggle when things go well for you? Are they lost for words if you get a great result in an exam, or a boy likes you? Do they seem to find it impossible to compliment you? None of these are good news.

2 THEY STEAL YOUR IDEAS . . .

and never give you the credit. It always surprises you when you see your friend wearing a dress you have or choosing a restaurant you liked. Because when they saw you wearing it, or spotted you tagging it in your stories, they told you how shit it was. If they put your taste down all day long, then rip you off behind your back, it's time to start waving the red flag.

3 THEY MAKE YOU DOUBT YOURSELF.

Let's set the scene. You arrive at a party, feeling all buoyed up by your new look and a glass of prosecco. Then you hear the whisper in your ear, 'Those trousers are really unflattering.' The wind is blown right out of your sails and somehow you find yourself going home at 9.30 p.m. Toxic behaviour strikes again.

4 THEY GIVE YOU BAD ADVICE TO STEER YOU IN THE WRONG DIRECTION.

On Monday morning you confide in your friend that you have a bit of a crush on James. By Monday lunchtime, they have told him and apparently he said you weren't his kind of girl. Six months later, you find out he's fancied you since Year 6.

THEY DELIBERATELY PUT YOU DOWN.

This can be on the micro level, the kind of jellyfish stings that someone else might not even notice, but these kinds of constant passive-aggressive digs can unravel your confidence. Examples: ' Oh babe, I don't think those shoes really suit you.' / 'I've got to be honest, that just does nothing for your calves.' / 'I think he's looking for a bright girl.' / 'I'd want someone to tell me if my dress looked that tight.'

THEY STEAL YOUR LIMELIGHT.

It's your birthday, everyone has brought you presents, and you're drinking champagne and getting pictures together. Suddenly your friend turns up and immediately bursts into tears over a spurious argument she's had with her on-again-off-again other half. Everyone forgets about you and rushes to comfort your weeping mate. It is toxic behaviour to need to be the centre of attention at all times.

THEY CONSTANTLY BITCH ABOUT OTHER PEOPLE TO YOU.

Someone who has always got gossip or a story is invariably a toxic friend. A busybody involved in everyone's business. A person who can't keep a secret and seems to get off on knowing more than you do about someone you both know. We all like a bit of celeb gossip here and there, but spreading bad news about people who are supposed to be your friends is a very different story.

IT IS NEVER, EVER ABOUT YOU.

The deep-seated insecurities which contribute to toxic behaviour exist independently from your relationship with a toxic friend. Those demons will follow them until they make the decision to do work on themselves. Ultimately, they deserve your sympathy, but that's probably better expressed from afar.

THEY KNOW WHEN TO TURN IT ON.

They can be a good friend when they need to be and they might not be toxic to other people, especially if they feel there is something to gain from them. In this way, they see the world as a hierarchy in which there are people above (whom they want to befriend) and people below (whom they often feel both superior to and threatened by).

What a good friend looks like

1. **GOOD FRIENDS HAVE HEALTHY BOUNDARIES.** We are so often told that a good friend is there 'no matter what'. But actually, that suggests that no matter how you treat your friends, they are supposed to suck it up. Instead we always say that good friendships have really clear boundaries and mutual respect. Yes, when you're going through a crisis you may sometimes lean more heavily on your friends, but never in a way that becomes unreasonable or disrespectful.

2. **GOOD FRIENDS ARE THERE FOR BOTH THE GOOD AND BAD.** Beware the fair-weather friend, but also remember that misery loves company. There are some people that only have the capacity to ride the highs with you, but there are also others who may thrive seeing you on the down – perhaps while you go through a break-up or navigate a difficult blip in your career. A great friend should share your joys and console your woes and never make you feel guilty for either.

3. **GOOD FRIENDS INSPIRE YOU.** Now, that doesn't necessarily mean they have to do something similar to you work-wise – it could be that they inspire you to go to a new workout class with them or take you to a new restaurant that they love. It could simply be that they inspire you to be a better, or wiser person. But there will be something that you admire in them and they feel the same way about you too.

4. **GOOD FRIENDS BRING YOU JOY.** When it comes down to it, you have a really good time with them. If you can't have a proper laugh about something, there is something going wrong.

5. **GOOD FRIENDS GIVE YOU ENERGY.** After spending time with them, you should never feel down, or bad about yourself because of something that was said. Instead, you should feel energised and uplifted and just want to spend more time with them.

6. **IT'S A TWO-WAY STREET WITH A GOOD FRIEND.** While dynamics and circumstances can change things over time, generally you should both be putting in the same level of commitment, time and energy into the friendship. Obviously, life happens, but the investment in each other should feel roughly equal. If it is always your friend doing the reaching out and organising, it's time to show her you care.

How to cope with being ditched by your friend(s)

1. TAKE TIME TO GRIEVE.

Just like the end of any relationship, it can feel brutal when a friendship breaks down, especially if it was a one-way decision. Don't be embarrassed to feel sad and hurt – that is so natural. Accept that it will be a process to come to terms with the loss of someone (or several people) that you cared about and thought had cared for you.

2. DON'T TRY TO SCORE POINTS.

When you feel like you've been dropped by a friend and let down, it can be very tempting to try to get some kind of revenge. But the only person that kind of toxic behaviour will hurt is yourself. Do your best to accept things in good grace and don't bitch after the fact. You may not be able to control losing your friend, but you can control the way you respond to it.

3. INVEST YOUR ENERGY IN NEW PEOPLE.

Remember that whenever someone walks out of your life, it leaves space for someone new. Instead of fostering any sense of bitterness or resentment, focus on meeting new like-minded people who share your interests and values. Friendships can't be forged overnight and often you meet people in the most unlikely of places. But putting yourself out there and choosing to do things that perhaps you might not have done in your old friendship is a sure-fire way of moving on with your social life and circle.

CHAPTER TWO

Starting Out & Building Up

When it comes to starting out in the world, it can feel like everyone has an opinion. From your teachers to your parents and friends, there can be lots of expectations about the steps that you take as you move into adulthood – especially when it comes to your career and university. Of course, some of the advice is invaluable – learning from others who have been through an experience already is massively important. But finding your own voice at this point of transition can be really, really hard. We get a lot of messages from you guys around the end of school or college saying how lost you feel and we couldn't empathise more, because it was a challenging time in our lives as well. The world can feel so intimidating, and your dreams and aspirations can feel incredibly unrealistic when you're at the bottom of the mountain.

In this chapter we wanted to share a little bit about how we got started in our careers. Before we go any further, we absolutely know we have so much more to learn and we are right at the beginning of that journey. We also acknowledge that we have been fortunate enough to have a lot of privileges that have enabled us to achieve everything we have at such a young age. We are white, cisgender, heterosexual women with supportive families who have always been in a financial position to support us. While there have been plenty of hurdles along the way, we know that we have had a head start and we never take it for granted. That is one of the reasons that we always say it's so important not to compare who has achieved x or y at this age or that age because, unfairly, we don't all start at the same start line. We are all on our own paths and everyone will go through more ups and downs than they can count before they get to a point where they feel that they have found their niche. And then everything might change all over again!

We wanted to tell some of these stories, because we didn't do what was expected of us at the end of school, and if we're honest we didn't really have a clue *what* we were doing. We took a lot of it day by day and tried to build our self-belief along the way. We worked minimum-wage jobs and then dedicated all of our free time to building something that we were passionate about on the side – our own thing that literally no one else cared about. It would have been easy to have seen what we were doing as pointless or hopeless, but we did whatever we could to keep positive and keep doing what we loved without any real idea of where it would lead.

We just focused on what made us the most happy, and one thing led to another in a way that no one, least of all we, could have predicted.

Rather than this being a list of dos and don'ts of what to do after school, we hope that what we went through just makes you think about exactly what it is that *you* want to do. There isn't just one route to your adult life, you don't necessarily need pieces of paper to progress and build a career. And just because you are young it doesn't mean that you can't build something for yourself. Hang in there, we promise it will all become clearer as you work your way through.

Dilemma One

I'm in my last year of A-levels and I can't work out what to do next. I have no idea what kind of job I'd like to do and most of the things I'm interested in don't seem to be the kind of things that can earn money. How did you guys know what steps to take at the end of school?

S: I really, honest to God, have never known what I wanted to do. Sure, when I was tiny, I used to say I wanted to be a teacher, but I've never known what I would be suited to. I suppose I've always known that I wanted to do something for myself, but I never really knew what that would look like – I mean, you're not taught any of that at school, are you?

When it came to GCSEs, then sixth form, everything at school became very tied up with which course you were going to go on to do at university and what kind of a career you wanted to pursue. Cinz and I felt so alienated from the whole process and conversation, and both of us in our heart of hearts knew we were going through the motions when it came to academics.

I do always remember my mum saying, 'Do whatever it is that makes you happy, and if you can turn your hobby into something that pays the bills, do that.' That absolutely stuck with me. Both of my parents were very enthusiastic about me getting into work – doing anything, from a paper round to waitressing. From the minute I legally could, I was earning – and Cinzia was the same.

C: Over the sixth-form years, we grew our bond as friends and found new ways to keep positive about the unknowns in the future. Whenever one or the other of us would have a wobble, we were always there for each other. We tried to have faith that everything would work out in the end and we didn't let other people pressure us into doing something we knew we didn't want to do. Whatever it was we *were* going to do, we knew we were going to do it together.

S: The first solid decision we made was that we were going to have a gap year. We wanted to spend some more time on our YouTube channel because we loved doing it so much and also dip our toes into the professional world to learn more about life outside the school gates.

C: I probably had a bit of a clearer intent career-wise than Soph, in terms of the fact that I knew I wanted to do something in the fashion industry after school. Both of my parents always fostered my creativity and our household never put academic subjects like Maths or Science on a pedestal. So, when I said I felt like I wanted to do something in fashion, they all thought it would be a good fit for me. I actually applied to do a fashion styling course in London. I knew I couldn't be a fashion journalist or designer, but I thought there might be a place for me in styling, whether that was for magazines or celebrities. Mum and I went down to London for an open day and as there was a low-grade requirement, I knew it was something that I could realistically do. I did end up getting a place and then I tried to persuade Sophia to get on the course too.

S: But I wasn't like Cinz, I hadn't done Art. See, I've always loved fashion and clothes, but I had no real interest in studying it.

C: I'm sure we could've talked you into the course. Anyway, I suppose in that sense, I did have a back-up plan. Although after we decided to take the gap year, I didn't go through the deferral process.

S: I think those conversations did crystallise this idea that what we were going to do would involve style in some way, though. I don't really know where my interest in fashion and beauty came from, because I always wanted to be like my brother.

As for my family, they were so encouraging and always supported me in pursuing anything I was interested in, from ballet to tae kwon do (yes, I really wanted to be like my brother). We have both been so lucky to have such supportive parents. I remember, around this time, my school rang my mum to tell her that I wasn't applying for university. 'Are you aware that she's not fulfilling her potential, or even trying to apply?' And Mum was like, 'Yeah, and?' She always said, 'Get an apprenticeship or a job, and start earning.' She was very practical. Neither of my parents, nor my brother, went to uni, so they didn't expect me to go either. But equally, if I'd been really into going to uni, they would have been hugely supportive of that too. It was more, don't just be a sheep and follow the crowd, think for yourself and work out if you do really want to spend three or four years of your life, and thousands of pounds, on something that won't fulfil you.

So, when we told them about our plan for the gap year, they were understanding. They agreed that it was worthwhile for us to take this year to get some experience and find a clearer path ahead.

C: Of course, we also had our part-time jobs. Sophia worked in retail and I worked at a club. That meant we had money to go out and live, and that's how we paid for any of the travelling we did over that year. But mostly in our free time we worked consistently at our content because we were having so much fun making it. It's easy to be dedicated when you truly love what you are doing, and by the end of school we'd managed to build up 10,000 subscribers, which wasn't a small achievement, because it's tough to get to that milestone.

We get a lot of dilemmas into the podcast about how to build a platform or become content creators like us. I always say the most important things are consistency and a real passion about whatever it is you are making content around – you have to be obsessed with it! Every single week of our gap year we uploaded videos and it took up the vast majority of our time outside of our part-time jobs to come up with that content. While we were having the time of our lives, it equally wasn't something that just 'happened' without any effort put in.

S: Equally, there was no 'agenda' when it came to making our content. Obviously, we hoped that people would see the videos and we wanted them to do well – but we weren't strategically following YouTube trends or anything like that. If we are both honest, as much as we both dreamt of a future that involved our hobby, we never really let ourselves dare to believe that it could become our full-time career. I think we really saw it as our side hustle. It didn't feel realistic to imagine anything else.

There isn't only one route into your adult life.

C: We weren't thinking about the next steps, or what our career trajectory could look like, or the range of opportunities it could bring us in the future. Because we didn't know what any of that was. We never imagined we'd have a podcast. Those kinds of things just weren't on our radar – I mean, I hadn't listened to a podcast before then, in all honesty. While we were really driven to make really great content that other people would enjoy, it was much more motivated by wanting to keep on doing what we loved, rather than building some kind of content empire!

Our part-time jobs were also *massively* important to us. That is really where we started to grow up and, for the first time, forge really positive friendships that we cherish to this day. Those jobs were the best things that ever happened to us and the atmosphere was just completely different to school, because there was such a mix of people from all different cities and backgrounds. Several of our new work colleagues were at uni and were older than us, and there was a different level of maturity in comparison to the cliques at school. They were also so supportive of what we were doing on our channel; everyone watched it and loved it. There was not a single note of negativity, which was so refreshing.

S: I remember being at work and thinking, *Wow, this is what it should be like.* I think the biggest thing was that we just had such a laugh. There were so many young people working in town, in all the shops and bars, and everyone would go out together after work, five nights a week. As soon as I got my ID, it was the best time, because we were always meeting people and rolling in this huge extended crowd. I think it was as close as we could get to a uni experience without actually going to one, especially as a lot of our friends were in halls.

C: I think it was a fresh start and it made us realise that there were other kinds of humans in the world outside of the school bubble. And of course, I worked at a club, so I was like, 'Come to my club and I'll give you free drinks! I'll sneak in a few of you, don't you worry!'

S: I'd always say to my work friends, 'My best friend works at this bar! It's great, we won't have to queue!'

While we were definitely doing plenty of playing, we were also working on some really fun, new content. Just before we left school, we had done a prom-themed *Get Ready With Us*, which our audience really liked, and we started to do more lookbooks, hauls and *GRWU* videos. We also made a lot of videos that, at the time, very few people saw – it wasn't like everything we put out was a success. I can remember the first time we made 10p from an affiliate link on a video [a link through to a product on which commission is earned if a viewer purchases it].

C: I was like, 'MUM! THIS MORNING THE BLOG HAS GENERATED 10P!!!'

S: And your mum would say, 'No, you've not.'

C: And we'd be like, 'YES, WE HAVE!!' Imagine!

S: For months and months, there wasn't much more to it than that. But slowly, we started to realise that our content could be more of a thing and that our consistency was gradually paying off. We started to speak to some of our peers and began to get the first inkling of what it might be like to work on YouTube as more of a job than a hobby. By the end of our gap year, we hit 100k subscribers. The magnitude of that achievement didn't really hit us for a long time, it's like we didn't quite realise that the dream was starting to become true. I think that was because so much of it was serendipity, rather than something we had mapped out in our minds, it had just all been so natural and fun that it was hard to comprehend. While you might think that your interests could never be something you could build a career around, until you try, you will never know. No one, us included, thought that it would do so well; it just shows you what can happen if you put yourself out there.

Dilemma Two

What are the pros and cons of working for yourself in your teens and early twenties? Does it get lonely?

S: We both love what we do with a passion and wouldn't have it any other way, but there is no such thing as a perfect job. Working for yourself is incredible, for so many reasons, but it can be quite insular – especially with YouTube, as we were either filming just the two of us, or alone editing.

C: That was one of the reasons it took us so long to leave our part-time jobs. We loved the camaraderie, and it was honestly such a good time.

S: But slowly, we started to reduce our hours until we were both only working a day a week. Our jobs were literally our entire social life and we knew if we left them, it would be very isolating, especially because we were so young. But of course, things move on, and lots of our friends at work finished uni, so they went off to their next jobs, and a whole new crew of people came in, and it just felt like the right time to hop out.

C: Another challenge when you're young and you work for yourself, is that you have had hardly any experience of the world of work, so you can be very naïve. I think that is one of the hardest things about setting something up on your own. Even though we were so inexperienced, we did try to be sensible and smart, and to think long term. We also asked a lot of people for advice along the way. So, when we were contacted by managers and agencies, people who were a lot older than us and already had successful careers, we really took our time to work out what to do. There were people who tried to dazzle us with dollar signs and promised the world. We're talking fully grown men telling teenagers they would be earning six figures 'next month'.

If we'd had less sensible heads on our shoulders, we might have been sucked in and that is something that I think everyone needs to be wary of. There are always going to be people in the world of business, no matter what your career, that are prepared to take advantage of you, and when you work for yourself as a young person you don't have much of a safety net.

S: A couple of months later, we were approached by the agency that we still work with today. Even though the conversations were much more positive, and there weren't the same red flags, we did still feel very out of our depth. We didn't fully understand what managers actually did, or what their role was. We were nineteen and twenty, so if we're being real, we didn't know up from down.

C: I mean, how are you meant to know? The only people we could talk to about it was our parents, and they had absolutely no experience of this kind of industry. In the end, we decided to go ahead, because there was a lot happening that we didn't have the tools to cope with. Working on legal contracts, negotiating deals, emailing back and forth with PRs when we didn't really know what we were saying or what we were agreeing to. If you set up on your own as a young person, it is really important to remember that you don't know everything. You have to be humble and be honest about what is beyond you and, if you can, look for support from someone who does have that experience.

But really, as much as there were (and are!) some challenges, we love working for ourselves and overall couldn't recommend it more. Whether you start your career on your own or work for a while in a more structured business before going out on your own, there are so many amazing things about being your own boss.

Be humble and honest about what is beyond you and look for support from someone who does have that experience.

Dilemma Three

I really struggle to get out of my comfort zone and I feel scared about doing nearly everything that I need to do to follow my dreams. How do you guys manage to always be so confident about everything you do?

S: Firstly, we are not always confident.

C: Definitely not! We also both sometimes get anxious about doing new things and that was especially true earlier in our careers.

S: I think now, looking back, we can see that there were so many sliding-door moments with our career, moments when we could have just chickened out and avoided doing something because it made us feel scared. But if we had, we would have missed out on so many incredibly special opportunities that have had a huge impact on where we are now. That is now such a big motivator for us to push ourselves out of our comfort zone – knowing that it always pays off in some way.

Like with our podcast, for example. It was not at all inevitable that we would go down that road. I remember around the time that we signed with our manager, people had started to talk more about podcasts, and we'd started to listen to them ourselves. We both brought it up to each other and we began to think that maybe it would be something we could be good at. But it was our management that really pushed us to make it a reality.

On our YouTube channel we'd started this series called *Boy Talk*. So often, we would get direct messages from girls asking us for advice on boys. On our *Get Ready With Us* videos, we'd always be talking about guys we'd met on a night out and recount what had happened, how we'd met, if we liked them, blah, blah, blah. We started to get a lot of messages from girls saying, 'I wish I had a best friend like you, I've got a bit of a problem.' Because girls were always asking us for advice on their love life, I remember thinking, *Why don't we do a video that's just us answering people's dilemmas?*

C: We were like, 'What shall we call it? *Boy Chat*? *Boy Issues*? What about *Boy Talk*? That's it!' We did those videos regularly, loads and loads of them, and then we thought perhaps it would be worth starting *Girl Talk* videos too, which focused on friendships, because we were also getting a lot of messages about the same kinds of problems that we'd experienced at school.

We got a lot of comments from our audience suggesting that we turn those videos into a podcast, so the universe was sending us signs from all directions. Podcast, podcast, podcast. Until we got to the point when we were like, 'We have to do this *now*.' I think that's why we just threw ourselves into it. We hadn't had time to freak ourselves out about it or talk ourselves out of it, but it was definitely really intimidating.

S: While A-cast [the largest global podcast company, which provides hosting, analytics and ads] guided us in terms of the structure (a great podcast has to have an identifiable beginning, middle and end, and it's helpful to have some kind of signpost for each, so people know where they are in the episode), the creative content all came from us – we didn't have anyone else in to build the concept or support us in any of that, and I think that's one of the reasons it has been so successful, because it really does come from our hearts.

C: On the first day recording, we arrived, sat down and the technician was like, 'Right, I'll just press play and you can go.' And he was just watching us and we were like, 'Ummmmm . . .' It was weird because we'd just walked in, we were totally cold, and it was something we had never, ever done before. But after that initial hesitation, we just launched into it, and we've never looked back. It has been so much fun, we have loved every single minute of every single episode. It's so funny, but it's like we were made to do this job – this job that we'd never heard of, all those years we were at school, and hadn't even dreamt of because we didn't know it existed. The best advice we could possibly give is really just to try new things out. No one has everything planned out and not everything you do is a massive, instant success. It's really easy to believe that other people have things all figured out and have this game plan that they follow with absolute confidence, when the truth is that nearly everyone feels just like you!

Dilemma Four

I'm taking a gap year, trying to get a lot of work experience together so I can try to get a paid job in television production. I don't know anyone from that world and it feels like I'm putting so much time and effort in and not getting anywhere. Do you think I should keep going or maybe it's just not for me?

S: I think the first question you have to ask yourself is are you enjoying yourself? Do you actually like the work you're doing on your placement or do you more like the *idea* of the job? When we first started out, it felt like we made all this effort and invested all of our money and free time in this dream without any reward. There weren't any likes or comments; no one saw any of it. For us, outside of our parents, there wasn't anyone else in our lives saying, 'This is great.' But we always loved every single part of creating content. But like you, we didn't know anyone in anything close to this industry either and it can definitely feel like there are a lot of closed doors.

C: I think that a lot of the success we have enjoyed came from the positive attitude we created in our gap year. From when we left school, whenever Sophia worried about anything to do with our future, I would constantly say, 'It's going to work out, we just have to keep passionate and keep going.' Of course, there was luck involved – with the timing in particular – but there is definitely something to be said for the power of chipping away towards creating something you love over a long period of time. And even though we were making a lot of positive moves along the way, don't get us wrong, we felt just like you're feeling now all the time.

S: Because in the background, there was always this thought, *Shit, what are we going to do if it doesn't become clearer which career we should pursue . . .* When you've gone out on a limb to do something out of the norm, it can feel like there is a lot of pressure for it to happen and for it to happen quickly. But the most important part of the whole thing is for you to have the opportunity to really work out if it is *actually* what you want to do. If you're not *actually* loving it, there is no shame in changing course. It's not embarrassing to take a risk and realise it's not right for you.

The energy
you invest into
work will often
blossom

in ways you
could never
have predicted.

C: Hand on heart though, we never had that feeling and we truly wanted to keep going with our content, regardless of whether it was successful or not. There was not one moment at that time that felt like a chore or a slog. It was just fun, we were obsessed with it. That doesn't mean there weren't moments when we questioned what we were doing. We could have thrown in the towel so many times.

S: But in the end, it was such a good lesson in humility and it also taught us that the energy you invest into work will often blossom in ways you could never have predicted. It's always worth putting in the hard work upfront, because eventually it will pay off, even if it's in ways you hadn't imagined. People will discover your work somehow, even if it's ten years later. Or else, all of your work will help you develop skills that will then take you on to the next level, somewhere down the line. At the beginning, it's so easy to give up, because it's incredibly time consuming and you're putting all this passion and energy into something and feeling like you're not getting anywhere, but if you love it, hang tight and keep going. You will get there!

Dilemma Five

A career like yours looks so amazing from the outside and I think I'd really love to pursue something in this industry too. Is there anything about your work life that you struggle with?

C: As we said above, there is no such thing as a perfect job. And working in any capacity online often comes with its well-documented challenges. In fact, being online full stop, whether it's work related or not, can come with challenges! From time to time we have had to learn to manage comments and messages that have been abusive and very unkind – something that, sadly, even young schoolchildren sometimes have to contend with in this day and age. Don't get us wrong, we think it sucks that anyone has to read this kind of thing, and it isn't something we have just been able to brush off every day. But, we do believe that you can't allow the negativity to win, especially when there is so much love and positivity out there.

Trolling and negative comments can make you question yourself whether you are a teacher in a school, an artist, or content creators like us. And of course, when your whole livelihood is based online, it can make it feel even harder to escape. We've had some pretty terrible messages about nearly everything you can think of by this point – body stuff, stuff about our looks, our relationships, our relationship with each other, our backgrounds, our intelligence . . . Nothing is off the table when it comes to online hate.

S: At the start, you'd read it and you couldn't disassociate yourself from it. I think we were embarrassed to even admit to each other how much it was getting to us. When you read something negative about your voice or your face or personality, the next time you have to stand in front of anyone in a professional environment, it can undermine your confidence. We get a lot of messages from you guys about dealing with online abuse, from trolling to harassment, and the one thing that everyone says is that when you read something negative about yourself, you can't help but latch on to it.

C: Fortunately, I think we've always been quite good at keeping it in perspective and contextualising the odd horrible comment. We are so lucky with our lovely, amazing followers and there is such a sea of love there, something that we never, ever take for granted. We have also learnt to manage online abuse and do everything we possibly can to avoid it. If you are ever in a situation where someone is sending you inappropriate, nasty or aggressive messages, never feel ashamed or alone – it is so incredibly common to go through something like this no matter what your job. You should feel empowered to use any digital tools to filter and block abusive words and block anyone who is using the online world to project their negativity on to you. Remember that it is *always, always, always* about them and not about you.

S: It's totally normal to feel upset and hurt if you have to deal with any kind of undeserved or aggressive criticism – whether that is online or offline. Like everyone, we go through peaks and troughs with our emotional response to it and while nine times out of ten we will be able to rise above, from time to time it does get to you and you might have a little cry. I think the most important thing – and this is especially true if you are really young and at school and dealing with anything remotely like cyberbullying – is to not feel alone with it. These messages can make you feel so alienated and isolated. And while yes, lots of people struggle with it, it is never OK. You should always try to find someone you can confide in about it.

C: For us, I can't remember there being one moment when we've been like, 'That's it, the haters have won, we can't do this any more.' And while I'm sure there are some corners of the internet out there saying spiteful things, I choose very intentionally not to seek them out. There are always going to be people who want you to fail, who find your success and happiness trigger deep feelings of discontentment in themselves – and that can be the case with people who have known you since you were four years old, as well as people who live on the opposite side of the planet and are generations older than you. Learning how to cope with that has been a huge part of our journey so far, but if you can free yourself from trying to please people who will never support you, or ever have your best interests at heart, you will find that the sky is the limit. Always remember that you just can't be everyone's cup of tea. You could be the juiciest peach in the world, but there will still be people out there who don't like peaches.

S: Nastiness can thrive in any work environment, and while the online element that we have dealt with is a little more visible, the lessons are the same no matter where or how it happens. I would never ever say that it should put anyone off following their dreams into a career in this industry, or indeed any other industry where your work is open to abuse.

C: Our career to date has been such a wonderful ride, and we are so proud of what we've achieved. Nothing is perfect, you don't get anywhere without commitment and hard work, and like any industry there are challenges to working in content creation, which we are still grappling with. But my God, we love our jobs! We know what an incredible privilege it is to do something that we are so passionate about, and we want to really honour that by taking every opportunity that comes our way and running with it.

Should you go to uni?

Quiz questions

1. If none of your friends were going to uni, would you:
Feel much more nervous about going? (3)
Be relieved? If they're not going there's less pressure on you. (2)
It makes no difference, you've applied to Aberdeen anyway. (4)
Consider recruiting them for your girl band? (1)

2. What is the number one reason you want to go to uni?
To get out of my city. (1)
I'm passionate about my subject and want to know more. (4)
I need to go to uni for my career path. (3)
The social life. (2)

3. What do you think your experience will be like?
A couple of years on the piss, with three months of insane
   cramming at the end. (3)
Life affirming and eye opening. I hope it completely changes my
   perspective on the world. (4)
Very hard work and probably a bit depressing. (1)
I haven't really thought about it. (2)

4. If you didn't go to uni, what would be your biggest worry?
Missing out on learning new skills and gaining knowledge that I'd
   never have the same chance to gain at any other time in life. (4)
Losing touch with my friends. (2)
Ending up in a job you don't really like. (3)
Other people thinking I'm stupid. (1)

5. Do you feel pressure from anyone to go to uni?
Yes, everyone seems to want me to go to, from school
   to parents. (1)
Career-wise there is no alternative. (3)
My friends all want me to go to uni. (2)
No, just myself! (4)

Scores

0–5: Probs not for you

Of course, there are wonderful opportunities to be found at university. But it seems very much that they are not for you. Several of your answers have suggested that the only reason you are interested in uni is because other people expect you to go, and you want to change your life. But there are so, so many ways to do that without doing something that you know will depress you. Be bold. You can be successful without a degree; you just have to believe in yourself.

6–10: Uni isn't just a social life

It's a hundred per cent understandable that you want to follow your friends and keep your relationships intact by ensuring you stay on the same schedule as your social group. But if being with them and having a good social life is the only reason for going to uni, you have to really think hard about it. The reality is that these friends may not always be around, so you shouldn't make big life decisions based on them. And if they are forever friends, they will still be there no matter what you decide.

11–15: Lukewarm learner

While uni may not be the defining moment of your life, it seems that you will probably enjoy several aspects of it, and it will help you along your chosen career path and enable you to reach your goals. Just remember, it is not the be-all and end-all, so if you struggle during term time, it is absolutely not the end of the world.

16–20: Uni queen

You were born to reach the loftiest heights of higher education! You go buy yourself a cute library bag, pack that pencil case and work on your UCAS application.

Uni is for you!

Successful women who don't have a degree

Oprah Winfrey – need we say any more?

Coco Chanel – raised in a convent, the orphaned and penniless Coco was educated by nuns, but that didn't stop her from becoming one of the richest women in the world.

Folorunso Alakija – the richest self-made woman in Africa, indeed the richest Black woman in the world, went to secretarial college after school and started out as a PA. Now a billionaire, she has several honorary doctorates, but no university degree.

Charlotte Tilbury – after just three months studying make-up, Charlotte launched her career as the world's most successful make-up artist. She recently sold the majority stake of her very own make-up brand for a reported $500 million.

Jessica Alba – Actress, founder and chairperson of Honest, a natural baby and beauty company valued at close to $1 billion. Also: megababe.

Anna Wintour – the devil in Prada didn't need three years in halls to become the most powerful woman in the fashion business.

Tyra Banks – the creator and executive producer of the juggernaut that is *America's Next Top Model* dropped out of university in her first semester to fly to Milan and Paris for fashion week. She was so successful, she never went back.

Kim Kardashian – while she may/may not still be studying for a law degree, Kim has done more than just break the internet, she's remade the world in her image.

How to cope with destructive criticism

DON'T TAKE CRITICISM (OR PRAISE) FROM SOMEONE YOU WOULDN'T SEEK ADVICE FROM. If you wouldn't respect their advice or value their opinion, don't respect their criticism. Unless someone knows you, wants the best for you and is qualified by your regard for them, their opinion is just not relevant.

ONLINE, PEOPLE CAN OFTEN GET A WARPED SENSE OF YOUR LIFE, NO MATTER WHO YOU ARE. They can imagine and conjure up a whole other version of your reality, and that is unfortunately out of your control. Any kind of online bullying is generally coloured by a person's insecurities, fears and traumas based on something they believe they see in you, whether it is true or not. If you don't know them personally, online criticism isn't personal. It only tells you about them. While it can be incredibly hard, you have to keep that constantly in mind.

ACKNOWLEDGE THE FACT THAT CRITICISM CAN BE NEGATIVE AND NOT AT ALL CONSTRUCTIVE. So often, we have been trained to see feedback as a gift, as a teachable moment or a way to help us better ourselves. But that is just not true in all instances. Sometimes criticism is just mean-spirited people venting their frustrations on you.

DO NOT RETURN TO DESTRUCTIVE CRITICISM, WHETHER IT'S SOMETHING THAT HAS BEEN SAID ONLINE OR IN A WHATSAPP MESSAGE OR TEXT. Delete any trace of it from your devices, burn the letters. Do not feed your insecurities, and the part of you that doubts yourself, with their negativity. Do not seek out destructive criticism in any context – and if you happen upon it, do not delve into it, however tempting it might be.

DON'T DIGEST HURTFUL, OFFENSIVE OR BULLYING CRITICISM. Don't continue your day processing their words. Keep your boundaries tight and protect yourself.

'Get Ready With Us' kit

NIVEA SOFT MOISTURISING CREAM – Rosie Huntington-Whiteley wears it on the red carpet and it costs less than a fiver. We use it everywhere (face, legs, elbows).

BEAUTYBLENDER – the only option for flawless base.

PORNSTAR MARTINIS – we prefer ours in a can, because who has the time to purée passion fruit?

MUSIC – Cody Simpson LOL.

MAC GIVE ME SUN! BRONZER – the one, the only.

BABYLISS CURLING WAND – for the perfect undone waves.

OUAI MATTE POMADE – if you're putting your hair up, this smooths it perfectly.

YSL BLACK OPIUM – we both always wear it.

AN OVERSIZED DENIM JACKET – vintage Levi's is the best (that saw us through a lot).

GOLD HOOPS – never, ever get old.

BLACK NAIL VARNISH – just to switch it up and keep things cool.

KIKO HYDRA LIPGLOSS – in 02 and 03.

A PLASTIC WATER BOTTLE – so you can transfer your pornstar martinis and drink them in the taxi. We're classy really. Hahahaha.

'There's something special and timeless about girls getting ready together.'

ERIN HEATHERTON

To:
_____

Subject:
_____

How to answer a professional email

Dial back the exclamation marks. Unless there's an exclamation mark in the name of the company, we'd suggest keeping your use to zero. Full stops all the way.

You can be direct. Don't beat about the bush, or try to go in too softly, softly. Provide the information and sign off. You can't put your personality in an email, so you might as well just get down to it.

Delete the 'Sent from my iPhone' at the bottom because that looks shit.

'Many thanks' or 'Kindest regards' are fine at the end. No kisses.

Check your spelling, and use paragraphs. Make sure you space everything out, but keep it brief and to the point. There's no need for your life story.

What to wear for a business meeting

AN OVERSIZED BLAZER IS YOUR BEST FRIEND. You can dress it up with a pair of heels in the evening to make it quite sexy, or you can make it more casual in the day, but it can still work for any formal environments.

DETAILS MATTER. Chipped nail polish and dirty hair are no-nos, because they just suggest that you don't take pride in your presentation, or that you don't respect the other people in the room. Neither is good.

GOOD QUALITY EVERYDAY JEWELLERY IS ALWAYS A GOOD INVESTMENT. For a long time, we just bought cheap jewellery from the high street. You'd have it for a couple of weeks, then your finger would turn green, so you'd have to go back and buy another one. It's worth saving up for simple pieces, like a pair of hoops that won't tarnish. You end up spending the same in the long run anyway.

IF MAKE-UP MAKES YOU FEEL CONFIDENT, PUT YOUR FACE ON. But just do what you would normally do. You need to feel comfortable, especially if there's the potential that you might have to make uncomfortable decisions in this meeting. You don't want to wear anything that is distracting for you or makes you fidget. That will help you to be more present – and enable you to focus on what you want to focus on, and not your outfit.

CHAPTER THREE

The First Cut is The Deepest

Is there anything more all-consuming than heartache? So often we receive distraught messages from our audience and sometimes when you read them all together, you can start to lose faith in love. Because it can be so brutal. We have had our hearts stamped on in different ways along the road and have also had to navigate moments when we were the ones doing the heart breaking. Quite often it feels like nothing is fair in love, especially when you are really inexperienced. Nothing seems to happen like it's 'meant' to, and when you are young it is so easy to miss some really glaring warning signs that a relationship is dysfunctional.

We are only a couple of steps ahead when it comes to understanding relationship dynamics, but we can already see how we made mistakes and so much of that comes from your own self-worth. When you have grown up believing that some of your value is based on how many boys like you, it is really easy to lose track of all the things that make *you* special *without* a boyfriend. Our biggest piece of advice if you are in a bad relationship right now is that you deserve so much more. Not 'you're better than him', or anything like that (though that may be the case). But more, you deserve to be happy on your own terms. We really hope that what we have been through can help you shine a light on some of your struggles – or if you can't identify at all with our stories, we hope that it will reiterate the truth that *everyone* faces obstacles in their romantic relationships at some point.

Dilemma One

I'm just about to finish school and I have next to no experience with boys. I've kissed a boy, once two years ago, but I've never had a boyfriend or anything approaching a sexual experience. I feel so embarrassed about it and also am starting to wonder why boys don't seem to find me attractive when so many of my friends are always being asked out on dates. What's wrong with me?

C: There is absolutely nothing wrong with you. Soph and I were exactly the same! Neither of us had a clue about boys at school, it was like they were an entirely different species.

S: The funny thing is that, when it comes to boys, I was actually a total tomboy growing up. I have a brother who is two years older than me, and I was always desperate to be like him. So, I did hang around with boys a bit when I was younger. When I reached my teens, I definitely learnt some lessons from my brother and his girlfriend in terms of what relationships were like. But that's about as far as it went in terms of actually knowing any boys. Considering how many of them there were in our school, it's almost unbelievable how little we found out about them.

C: I was the complete opposite to Sophia, because I'm the eldest of three sisters and grew up in such a female-dominated house. As a little girl, I dreamt of being a ballerina. I've always been very into hair and make-up and all the glamour – let's just say I was not going to tae kwon do with Soph! When it came to school, though, we were pretty much in exactly the same boat with boys: clueless and not particularly interested. We were definitely not boy mad, and we pretty much kept ourselves to ourselves. My first true love was Cody Simpson, so when I looked at all the boys at school, I just thought, these boys are nothing like Cody. He really gave us false expectations.

S: We did have some boys as friends, and from time to time we fancied particular boys. There was this one boy that I really fancied all the way through primary school and we were 'boyfriend– girlfriend' for about a week in Year 6, even though we never spoke to each other. Then I fancied this other boy from Year 7 to Year 11, but it was unrequited, because he had this thing for another girl. Occasionally I'd be 'talking' to a boy, so I'd have a kind of 'boyfriend' for a month, but I didn't really ever spend any time with them or anything. It was never a relationship. Sixth form was an absolute desert – actually no boy interests at all – because we were both like, *No, thank you.* There were girls at school who were in full-on relationships and would spend time at their boyfriend's house, and we never had anything like that. But I don't remember ever being particularly sad about boys while I was at school, we didn't really entertain the idea that much.

C: We were definitely late bloomers. I didn't kiss a boy until I was seventeen.

S: I was fifteen, it was at a house party.

C: We weren't in a rush to lose our virginities at all. I suppose we were a bit of an anomaly because we just weren't that fussed about romance. Look at my sister Lidia, for example. She has been in a proper relationship since she was fourteen. She was with her first boyfriend for three years and then she was in another relationship during sixth form for two years. And that was just never me or Sophia. Which is bizarre, I suppose, because I do think it's more common when you go to a mixed school to have some kind of relationship with a boy at some point.

S: Well, it wasn't like we were batting them off with a stick, was it?

C: True.

S: Because we had such a close friendship, and we'd get home and just turn on music and FaceTime each other on our iPads all night, I think we never really felt the need for a boyfriend. I think also because both of us were permanently single, it didn't matter. Maybe if Cinzia had had a serious boyfriend, I might have felt more pressure to find one for myself.

C: We get so many emails in like yours worrying about not having had any experience with boys, especially if they're going to uni. Most often, they're scared people are going to judge them, or it will be a big deal that hangs over their head. Every time I read something along these lines, it always makes me upset because there is just no rush.

S: We do get a lot of that, and we always say, it will happen when it happens. It's just not a race.

C: There is so much pressure from school especially. A lot of the girls we knew in our classes were already sexually active and sleeping with boys and it was hyped as a really big deal. I think we were a bit scared and intimidated, which is maybe another reason why we didn't engage in the whole boy craze.

S: I'm so thankful that neither of us felt any pressure to lose our virginity.

C: When it did happen, it wasn't a good experience, it wasn't a bad experience, it was just what it was. It wasn't momentous. It was nothing special, but nothing sordid. That's what we try to say on the podcast in terms of expectations around virginity and first sexual experiences. You're most probably not going to have this incredible fireworks moment, whether the guy is your one true love or someone you're more loosely seeing. Either way, early experiences can be a bit surreal, awkward and underwhelming.

S: **Even though everyone has been talking about it all for years and years. And then it happens, and you can feel a little bit detached from it. But it would be disingenuous for me to say that it doesn't change anything at all. I do think it gives you a bit more confidence going into other relationships, simply because of the way that you are conditioned, at school and beyond, to see it as this rite of passage.**

C: Afterwards, you don't feel *totally* inexperienced. But really, it doesn't matter at all. All that matters is that you're with someone who loves you and keeps you safe. All this pressure about needing experience, and having all these moves and skills and all this knowledge going into a relationship, is just rubbish. None of that's important. What's important is to make sure this person is actually nice to you first and that you're a good match.

Dilemma Two

I've just started dating a boy in my local town. I've known him for a while and from the moment I first saw him, I really fancied him. Sometimes he seems to really like me, and we have fun on our dates, but other times he is quite distant, and he doesn't always answer my messages. I feel like I don't know how to act, I'm not sure if we're on the boyfriend–girlfriend path and I don't want to put him off.

C: After we left school, everything changed for us with boys almost overnight. I remember when I got my job at the club, all the guys were just so fun. I built these great platonic relationships, and they were all so supportive of everything we were doing. I remember being like, *Jesus, this is great*!

S: That was the same for me at my shop; everyone I met, both girls and guys, were so supportive of us. It's probably not surprising in retrospect that I met my first boyfriend there. Like you mentioned in your dilemma, I remember being totally and completely dazzled by my boy when we first met.

C: Even when you first started that job, you'd say, 'There's this guy here, he's *gorgeous*.' You'd never seen anything like it. 'He's like, a model, come in and look at him. He's *older*.'

S: Yeah, he was a few years older than me, which felt massive at the time. I remember seeing him at work and thinking that he would never look at me twice. When you're at school, the only boys around you are in your year, aren't they? Even having a boy in the year above fancy you was huge. So, having a guy who was so much more 'mature' be interested in me was like, *Oh my fucking God. How have I managed this?* In hindsight (isn't it a wonderful thing?), I was far too focused on the more superficial side of things, like his age and how handsome he was. I also couldn't get over the fact that he liked me. I liked him because he liked me, and I hadn't ever been used to that.

   He was definitely a player and at the beginning he was very changeable with me – and of course, that only made me want the relationship to work out even more. I was just eighteen when we started, and I remember when we got together thinking that it would probably only last for the summer, because then he'd be off looking for another girl. But somehow it kept going. There was some kind of idea that we might break up after around the year mark, and I was really upset, because at that point I really wanted to be with him, but it didn't happen.

Even though I was infatuated, I do remember thinking, even at the beginning, *Do we have that much in common?* I don't really know what we spoke about, and we didn't really laugh that much. We'd have a great time at work with the group, but then when it was just the two of us, there wasn't much of a deeper connection.

C: I guess I could say the same on that count too. I also met my first boyfriend at my work.

S: Well, remember you had that guy who worked in town first. You had a few bad eggs in a row at the beginning.

C: That's so true! With that guy, it was my first time seeing anyone and we'd go on dates all the time. We'd go to the cinema and get drinks, at least once a week for a good while. He'd call me all the time, but nothing was really progressing – as you say, it's that thing when you're like, are you my boyfriend? Or am I meant to be dating other boys too? It was weird and I didn't really know what was happening, because of course, it was my first experience. Sometimes we'd see him on nights out, but he never made it clear what he wanted. He ended up telling me he didn't want to see me any more, and I was devastated. I hadn't really thought about what was going on, then suddenly he just cut it all off and didn't want to speak me. I really did feel heartbroken, it was my first real rejection, even though we weren't even boyfriend–girlfriend.

S: Well, you could have been, the amount of time you spent dating him. At the time, we were just trying to figure it all out as we were both getting really mixed signals. It felt like the whole thing was an absolute minefield. In contrast to Cinzia, my boyfriend-to-be never asked me out on a date, it was always more like, 'Come and meet me and my friends.' I'd turn up and everyone would be drinking. Later, he'd put his arm around me, but there was no hint initially of us taking any more steps. I just didn't know what to make of it all, what the timeline should look like, what any of the rules were, or how the hell I was meant to 'play' any kind of game.

C: We were genuinely like, 'What the F is going on?! These boys, they're not direct at all, how are we meant to know what they want?' If we'd had *any* experience, we would have spoken up for ourselves, and looking back we would have handled things *way* differently. Those relationships probably wouldn't have even happened.

I liked him because he liked me, and I wasn't used to that.

S: But back then, the boys called the shots, and you went along with what they wanted to do.

C: I know. I think we were just so naïve and overwhelmed. It was, 'This boy likes me! This boy likes me!' That was enough. And then, 'I *need* you to keep liking me.' Because oh my God, if you stop liking me, Jesus Christ that is going to be terrible.

S: We were absolutely seeking validation from these boys. I would do or say whatever I thought they wanted me to, just so they would like me. We would always try so hard to be 'super chill' with our boyfriends, because I remembered my brother and all of his friends always complaining about high-maintenance girls. So, we felt we had to be super relaxed, not get on their nerves, and just make their lives easy. I can so remember that feeling of not wanting to chase him away.

C: We just wanted to please too much! And that's just not right.

S: Half the things that happened at the start of my relationship, today I'd be like, 'You can fuck right off!' But at the time, it was, 'No problem, I'm Sophia, I'm not like other girls, I'm super chilled! You do you, it's fine with me!'

C: Almost straight after that first dagger to the heart, I met another guy. And I kid you not, I thought I was going to marry him. We'd gone to the club we always went to on a Sunday night, and I walked in, and I remember seeing him and thinking, *Oh my fucking God, he is absolutely gorgeous. Who is this man?* I walked straight over to him – there might have been a few pre-drinks involved – and said, '*You*, you are *so* gorgeous.' We immediately hit it off and ended up properly snogging in the club, *bleugh*. The shame. Anyway, we exchanged numbers and I remember going home to my mum and being like, 'I met this boy last night, he is *amazing*!'

S: You messaged me saying that you'd met your husband last night.

C: I fell so hard that, within the space of about two days, I was completely besotted with him. And look, we did end up going on loads of dates and had a really good time together. We laughed so much, and it wasn't difficult for me to kid myself that it was going to go somewhere.

S: But you bent over backwards for him.

C: Yeah, I would have done whatever he asked me to. I completely lost myself in the whirlwind and idea of this romance.

S: It would be the end of his shift at like 3 a.m., and you'd be like, 'Right, I'm going to get up at half two and go and meet him after work.' And I was like, 'Are you all right, Cinz? What are you doing?!' WTAF!

C: Right. Then the issue became, why am I not this boy's girlfriend? What is going on? And that was my first 'what are we?' experience. He's not said I'm his girlfriend, but he still wants to see me all the time, and this has been going on for a while. It all ended when he straight out said that he didn't want to go out with me properly. While we'd only been seeing each other for four months, it really rocked me to my core. He was so good with his words, telling me that I was the one for him and that he'd never met anyone like me, but then his actions just did not support what he was saying.

S: What he wanted was a friend with benefits. I remember coming to yours and we were putting the world to rights, as usual. And you were like, 'He says he still wants to see me, but doesn't want to be girlfriend–boyfriend.' And I remember you were kind of thinking, if you still got to see him, maybe it was worth it. And I remember thinking *no*. Absolutely not. That is him saying, 'I really want to sleep with you, but I'm going to sleep with Sarah and Becky at the weekend as well.'

C: If I was treated today how that boy treated me then, I'd be out of that door in a second. Because I know my worth now. But when you're young and inexperienced, you're thinking, *Is this how it is? Is this what I deserve? Is this how things normally go in the beginning?* You just don't know, because you've never been through it before.

S: So much of it was the naïvety of not having the faintest idea of what a healthy relationship looked like, or how it was supposed to work. We didn't know what was and what wasn't OK . . . and we didn't really have a gauge of what being treated well was. I do think that you have to go through some of this heartache to really understand what a good relationship is. We could tell you a hundred times over, but when you are in that place with a boy, it's so difficult to take anyone's advice or get any perspective. All we can really tell you is to keep reminding yourself that when something is really right, you don't have to question it and that you are valuable and amazing and there is someone out there who will see that a mile off and appreciate you for all you are, inside and out.

Dilemma Three

Around my friends and family, I'd say I was a pretty confident person, but around boys, I become so shy and insecure. I have a lot of body issues and now I'm in sixth form, I feel like they are really standing in the way of getting to know any boys. You two always seem so sexy and confident, did you always feel like that?

S: I think when we look back, a lot of the bad behaviour we put up with from boys when we were younger was because we were still finding our feet in terms of our own self-esteem. I would say that we were always pretty confident on the outside, but inside we were definitely not anywhere near as secure as we are today.

C: In terms of boys, we weren't confident in ourselves because we just didn't know *ourselves* in a relationship. And we were still growing up and coming to terms with things like, are we adults yet? That moment in between school and adult life can be a really tough one.

It's true that we all have our awkward moments when we are growing, when you feel like the ugly duckling and maybe you haven't come into yourself yet, and that time can be difficult and make you feel insecure about your looks. We all blossom at different times and it's easy to look at other girls at school and the comparison can be really difficult. I definitely know that feeling.

We want to reassure you that things do improve on that journey and as you get older, and get to know yourself more and realise that the way you look isn't everything, you can release some of those negative feelings and that can help you increase your confidence across the board, not only with boys.

S: You have so much more to offer than just the way you look, and while that journey to self-acceptance isn't easy at all, you will get there.

C: There is a lot of pressure on young women around looks, and the accessibility of things you can do to make changes to your appearance can seem like the magic answer.

S: It's your body, your choice, and we support any woman who decides she wants to make a change to the way she looks. BUT, it is so important to understand that the kind of confidence that you are craving comes from within. Fillers, Botox, cosmetic surgery – it's all a personal choice, and as long as you are doing your research and not taking it lightly, more power to you. But it is not the quick fix that it seems to be at all.

C: I think it's so important to also realise that everyone has insecurities. I do really understand body issues, because when I left sixth form, my weight really yo-yoed. Even when I lost a lot of weight and was much smaller, I still felt like I was overweight. That's one of the most insane things about getting so caught up with your body like that – you can't even see what's in front of you in the mirror any more. Of course, like everyone, I still have moments even today, but I've never felt those extreme feelings about *needing* to lose weight again in quite the same way and you might find that your body hang-ups subside over time. People might not talk about their insecurities, but everyone is dealing with them in some form, especially when they are young.

S: I think that one thing that is really worth saying is that you won't find the validation you are craving from anyone but yourself. If you think boys don't fancy you, so that means you're not attractive, you are looking at it the wrong way around.

C: If you go out and no boys talk to you or you don't get any attention and some of your friends do, it can make you feel insecure and as though you must be unattractive, but that is just not the case!

S: It's your personality that makes you great.

C: Your quirks and your uniqueness.

S: That is what is the most attractive thing of all, so loving all the different sides to yourself is what you should be most focused on – not getting a boy to like you.

Dilemma Four

My best friend started seeing a new boy about four months ago and I feel like I've totally lost her. She hasn't made any effort to introduce me properly to her boyfriend, I've not really got any idea of what he's like or what they do together, it's like I've been totally cut out. I don't really want to say anything to her about it, because I know she will probably just think I'm being jealous. Should I bring it up or not?

C: Fairly soon after my 'husband' made it clear he wasn't the one, I had become aware of one of the guys that worked at my club. Every single girl seemed to fancy him, and I thought he was super handsome. He was at uni and, again, older than us. When we'd work on the bar together, all the girls were always asking for his number, and I would watch him take them home and be constantly flirting with women. Then all of a sudden, he started to pay me a lot of attention and I was really flattered. This is the guy that everyone else fancies and now he fancies me. Wow, that felt good. Like Soph, I didn't really consider whether he was a good match, or even a very nice person. Quite quickly, he asked me to be his girlfriend and because that had never happened to me, it felt like a big deal because I'd been starting to think that perhaps I wasn't *girlfriendable*. I remember feeling a massive sense of relief, and I guess security, because finally someone wanted me. It felt like I could relax. Looking back, I got into that relationship because that boy was universally wanted by other women and his attention had reassured me that I wasn't totally unwantable. I managed to completely gloss over the fact he wasn't good for me at all. After an amazing first six months, it turned sour.

S: What is wild is that I never knew about any of this, at the time. That relationship was so private, and I felt completely locked out of it. I'd known a lot about the other guys, but then when you two got together, there were no details. In hindsight, that was a major red flag, but as I hadn't experienced that kind of thing from the perspective of a friend, I just presumed that it must all be amazing because you never complained about it at all. From the outside it did look like true love, so I didn't want to rock the boat between us by asking otherwise.

C: After we'd been together for a year, things started to get more serious, but I was already having private doubts.

S: Obviously, Cinz and I are as tight as friends can get, but things did feel different between us. But then, I also thought, *Well, maybe this is just us going into adulthood.* I had my relationship, she had hers. Like, she has other things to think about and that's normal because we're adults now. It was a weird point in our friendship for sure.

C: I think it's because I knew, deep down, it wasn't a good relationship. Looking back, I'm like, oh my gosh, it was so terrible, I just can't believe it. What an idiot I must have been to have done that and put up with all of that. Of course, in the early months, we had good times. That's why you stay. But after a few months, it was just constant conflict and turmoil. I think, as women, we can make so many excuses for what your partner does or says. You feel so much pressure to stay and the desire to make it work, that you can leave your happiness to one side.

At the beginning, all I tried to do was please him. There was that security of being someone's girlfriend, and when things got tough, initially I'd hark back to the early days. This was my first relationship, and I didn't have the self-assurance to see the bad parts for what they were – inexcusable! I felt I couldn't tell anyone because they'd think less of me or him. I didn't want my friends and family to know the truth because I was ashamed. For anyone who is inexperienced and in a similar situation, just know that a relationship shouldn't be a dark secret and you shouldn't be feeling hurt, overwhelmed or sad most of the time. You should be talking to your friends and sisters about your relationship – don't ever let anyone make you believe you have to keep your pain to yourself.

S: What is weird is that even though I never had that much to do with him, there were so many signs that something was off. The fact I didn't know him. The fact that our boyfriends didn't hang out. The fact that you were so distant. But because I thought you were OK and happy and you both looked so happy on Instagram, I didn't mention my feelings. I didn't know how it would have sat with you if I'd aired my gut instincts. Again, I didn't have the tools to ask the right questions. There is obviously a line we all draw, when sharing aspects of our relationship with our friends. We all want our friends to like our boyfriends. I mean, of course, you can say he's being a fucking dickhead from time to time, but more

It's your personality that makes you great – don't change it for a boy.

difficult experiences can feel like too much to share. As a friend, I've realised it's important to ask the deeper questions. Sometimes people do need a nudge to share, and if they say no then you have to respect their boundaries. Of course, there is that honeymoon period in every romance, and your friend isn't going to be as available as she once was. But if she totally drops out of your life and becomes guarded about her boyfriend, it's definitely worth at least approaching her and letting her know you are still there for her if she wants to talk, no matter what.

C: There came a point in that relationship, when I stopped trying to always please him and started to push back, and that's when things got really difficult. I hated confrontation, I would never argue, and most days I felt so stuck.

S: Around that time, there had been a lot of changes and adjustments all happening at once. It had been a period of total flux and things had gone at a hundred miles an hour.

C: I think it was a combination of growing up, having these complicated and difficult experiences in our relationships, and that natural thing that happens after school with friends as you try to find your own way in life. It all happened so quickly.

S: We get a lot of girls writing in saying, my best friend has a boyfriend now and things aren't the same. They've changed, we've changed. And yeah, that happened to us too. But now we understand that strangeness between us was a symptom of being in the wrong relationships. I do think that leaving our part-time jobs and becoming full-time content creators was another part of that flux too. We were taking our work more seriously and we had managers, so it felt like there was more responsibility. We also went through a phase of feeling a bit lonely because we weren't going out with our friends all the time. We had this job that was so public, but also isolating, because we were so often at home on laptops by ourselves.

C: I personally feel like there were too many changes all at once and that I couldn't assimilate them all properly. There was a lot of negativity swirling around me and I felt like I couldn't even confide in my best friend.

S: That was a massive lesson for us in communication. Communication is everything in every relationship. If we'd have talked to each other about all of it, things might not have got so bad. Hindsight is great, but growing up can be tough sometimes and you don't always get everything right.

C: That's the most growth either of us had ever been through really. It was the best thing, in retrospect, but painful as hell at the time. There is always the chance that it is just the natural time to close the door on your friendship for now so you can step through to the next thing, which is so painful, but so normal and common. Or perhaps your friend is going through something completely different to what you're imagining. The only thing you can do is focus on yourself and all the other positive things in your life while keeping those lines of communication open as best you can.

Dilemma Five

I have been with my boyfriend for nearly eighteen months. Everything was so much fun at the beginning, and I thought that I was so in love with him that I literally wanted his babies. But over the past six months, I've found myself feeling so low and lonely in the relationship. It doesn't feel fun any more, we don't seem to click or have many of the same interests or ambitions for the future. I hate myself for feeling bored and trapped when he is actually a really sweet guy and he can't help who he is. I often find myself snapping at him and saying unkind things, but I feel like I can't leave because it will break his heart. What would you do? I feel like such a bitch.

S: This one feels really close to home for me and I really empathise with you. Unhealthy relationships where you aren't fulfilled are hard to find a way through. For the first six months of one of my relationships, it was all me doing the chasing. Then when we did get into the relationship, everything just coasted along without much drama. He was, and I'm still sure is, a lovely boy. He was lovely to me; he has a lovely family. But we were a mismatch. I remember during the second half of the relationship, the power dynamics started to switch, and it was my ex who really wanted to be with me, while I started to feel more lukewarm about things. I just thought, *Oh my gosh, I'm not happy in this relationship, I feel incredibly unfulfilled. But there's no horrible drama or unpleasantness, so I should stay, right?*

I would swing from thinking one way about it to the exact opposite a few days later, it felt like I couldn't connect with my inner voice. I ended up writing a letter to myself on my birthday and promised myself that if I was still having these doubts in a year, I had to end it. I think this is a great idea to figure out if your feelings are temporary or more entrenched. For example, sometimes you can feel bored in a long-term relationship and that's totally normal for, say, a month or so, but if you are feeling the same way six months down the line, it is likely reflective of a deeper issue.

I wish I'd set a shorter time frame for my feelings, because I went *another whole year* in a relationship that I was deeply unhappy in. Part of plodding along was comfort and routine. But part of it was also because there was nothing terrible about the relationship. He

Communication is everything in every relationship.

could be so generous and kind. I remember saying to myself, I could just stay with him and make him happy, even if I wouldn't be that happy, overall it would be OK. If we just stayed together for ever, it wouldn't be the worst thing in the world. I should be grateful that I have someone who loves me, right? I do also remember just thinking to myself, I wish he'd cheat on me or be horrible to me to give me a 'proper' reason to break up with him. As if my own happiness wasn't a valid reason. This feeling of unfulfillment and disconnection just did not feel like a significant enough reason to end a relationship. He wasn't doing anything wrong, but the truth is, that's not the same as it being right.

C: You can't stay with someone *just* because they're nice.

S: Even though I had emotionally checked out of my relationship, I felt a massive weight of guilt hanging over me. I knew that it had got to the point where I was in the wrong for letting it carry on. When I eventually broke it off, understandably he was completely blindsided, because I hadn't communicated any of my feelings for at least six months. From his perspective, it was like I was just throwing in the towel on our relationship, even though I had been trying so hard to make it work under the radar. I had brushed it all under the carpet, internalised it and kept it to myself. That's what I tend to do – because I feel like I should be able to deal with things on my own.

C: I think we're both like that.

S: I'm not very good at opening up and sharing the load. If I'm feeling shit, most often I don't want to talk about it, and I'd prefer to sit with the problem myself and mull it over. And that is something that I'm now working on, because it is not a good foundation for any kind of relationship. After my initial conversation with my ex, there was a big feeling of shock, and relief, but there was also, *Shit, was that the right thing to do? I've done it now, there's no going back.* I had that moment of F.U.C.K. But almost immediately it passed, and it was replaced by this incredible feeling of lightness. It was an instant weight off my shoulders because I had been carrying so much guilt. I knew what I'd been doing wasn't OK, and that he deserved to be with someone who absolutely was sure about the relationship and adored him. Putting yourself first can feel like the hardest thing to do, but it's something you have to do for your happiness, because if you're not happy, in the end you will never be able to make the other person happy either and they deserve so much more than that too.

While these struggles in your romantic life can feel crushing, you do also have to see the value these difficult early relationships can add to your life. Bad first relationships can actually set you up for really healthy, positive relationships in the future because they teach you what you don't want.

C: There isn't one perfect, straight road to happiness. You have to go through situations that aren't right to learn what *is* right for you. Figuring out what you don't want is just as important as working out what you do.

S: When people ask you, 'What are you looking for in a partner?', you can say, 'Six foot three, funny guy, well dressed . . .'

C: OK, sure, so he's all these things, but is he also controlling? Is he manipulative? Does he gaslight you? He may be handsome, but is he also cheating on you? These are things you might look past in the beginning because you are so focused on the ticks that he does have on your list that you completely bypass the red flags that you absolutely do not want.

S: You need to have at least a mental list of the traits and behaviours that absolutely will not work for you. So, when those things come to light, you don't just think, oh, I can look past that because he's loyal or kind, for example. You can stop and say, actually, he is displaying three traits on my 'I do not want' list and this isn't going to work in the long term. It's far easier to spot them when you identify them.

C: If you've ever gone through a situation where you've been left feeling deflated or broken hearted, like we have, just know that it is actually just another necessary step on your path to finding the right person – none of it, even the worst heartbreak, is for nothing.

S: The one thing you can really try to hope for when you have been through a really difficult time in a relationship is that you will never go through it again. You will know what you won't settle for again. If you hadn't had that experience you might not notice the warning bells the second time around. If you find you keep repeating history with bad decisions in relationships, it's probably time to step back and assess what is happening. The universe will send you the same messages until you take in the lesson. Until you realise what you need to avoid you may very well find yourself caught in a cycle of repeated bad choices for yourself.

C: Taking time after the end of a dysfunctional or unsuccessful relationship is so important for that very reason. You need that moment to digest what happened and the chance to find some clarity. Immediately jumping straight back into something might mean you miss that sign.

You need to look inward and not just consider which traits were wrong for you in your partner, but also your own behaviour. You can learn from every experience and mistake. The breakdown of a relationship isn't a failure on anyone's part – it's a teaching of a lesson to take forward into the next relationship and a necessary step towards finding the right person. If you don't pay heed to those lessons, you will probably find yourself repeating the negative patterns.

S: When you've not had any experience, you think you know what you want and what you don't want. You think you know what a nice guy is like and of course you want a nice guy. But the truth is perhaps you thrive more with a partner who challenges you in a way that your imaginary nice guy might not. Potentially you are best suited to someone who comes with opinions that aren't exactly the same as yours. Perhaps it's going to be that tension that creates a wonderful relationship for you. That is why you cannot be afraid to take the plunge and try all sorts of relationships, no matter what the risk of heartache. It really does take time for anyone to work out their perfect match, and inevitably in that process of trial and error, there will be some bumpy moments along the road – but they are all essential turns on the road leading you to your future happiness in love.

The Ten Commandments: for helping a friend considering a break-up

1. The number one rule here is to let your friend come to you. Be kind and gentle in your approach and never be too opinionated.

2. You don't want her to feel like you know better, or that you are pushing her into a corner, because then you risk being shut out completely.

3. You also don't want her to feel that you only come with negativity, or that you are trying to make her decision for her. You can't bully someone into making the right decision.

4. Never make her feel that you are personally invested in her leaving her partner, or that that is what you want.

5. Even if you really feel that this person is not of good character, offer him the benefit of the doubt and highlight his positives as well as his negatives.

6. Try never to say something that will create a barrier between you if she decides to continue with her relationship.

7. Always assure her that she is on a journey with her decision, and she doesn't have to make her mind up in that instant.

8. Speak about the issues in broad terms rather than making it too personal, and lay the facts out for her.

9. Ask her what she would say to you if you were coming to her with the same list of facts. What would be her advice if things were reversed, and it was you asking for help?

10. Ensure she knows that, whatever decision she makes, you are there for her. You're not there to judge, and whatever she decides, you will back her.

How to break up with someone

BE HONEST. Our overall philosophy when it comes to break-ups is that honesty is the best policy, and while it might not feel like it, the cold-turkey, direct approach is the kindest.

BE CONFIDENT. If you are a hundred per cent sure of your decision, the most important thing is that you stand your ground. Before you start the conversation, give yourself a bit of a pep talk, and keep in mind that when you go to bed that night it will be over with.

BE CLEAR. It is very important that you are not passive and that you use your language to express that. 'I have decided,' rather than, 'Perhaps we should?' Make it clear that you have been through a thought-process and come to a conclusion. You have to say the actual words: I don't want to be with you any more. Own your decision.

BE DIRECT. Don't pose your decision as something that is up for debate or discussion. There can't be a question.

DON'T TIPTOE. Don't leave anything up in the air. Don't say, 'Maybe in the future things might change.' Or, 'I'll reach out to you in a few days to see how you are.' Instead make it clear that you feel this is what is best for the both of you, and there is no changing your mind. Firm, direct and final.

CUT THE COMMUNICATION. After you have had the conversation, don't check in on them. If you care about them and their feelings, you cannot keep in contact, because you are only giving them false hope – and ultimately that is cruel. The last thing you need when you're trying to get over a relationship is to hear from your ex. That takes you right back to thinking they care about you, and you can build that up to be a sign of something so much more.

What to do if you think your partner may be abusive

From time to time, we will get a dilemma sent to us which we feel details an abusive relationship. We speak so much about toxic relationships, which of course can be hugely damaging, and we absolutely don't want to minimise that. But abusive relationships are where you feel that you have lost control of your own life and you feel you are unable to make your own decisions. The abuse is deliberate and calculated. Gaslighting, sexual abuse, emotional abuse and physical abuse are all about power and control – another human taking over your experience of life.

We always recommend that anyone who feels they might be in this situation should contact professionals for support. For women, you can call Women's Aid and Refuge, for men the Men's Advice line, and for LGBTQIA+ relationships, contact Galop for advice. Details can be found below.

The Freephone National Domestic Abuse Helpline, run by Refuge, on 0808 2000 247, is available 24/7. The staff will offer confidential, non-judgemental information and support.

Men can call Men's Advice Line on 0808 8010 327 (Monday and Wednesday 9 a.m. to 8 p.m.; Tuesday, Thursday and Friday 9 a.m. to 5 p.m.) for non-judgemental information and support.

If you identify as LGBTQIA+ you can call Galop on 0800 999 5428 (Monday, Tuesday and Friday 10 a.m. to 5 p.m.; Wednesday and Thursday 10 a.m. to 8 p.m.) for emotional and practical support.

Anyone can call Karma Nirvana on 0800 5999 247 (Monday to Friday 9 a.m. to 5 p.m.) if they are concerned about forced marriage and honour crimes.

There are steps you can take to help avoid being drawn into an abusive relationship, though it's important to say that anyone can find themselves in a bad situation.

Recognise the red flags and don't ignore them

Because we're romantics and we want to fall in love, we can excuse a lot of bad behaviour right from the beginning of a relationship, without realising it. Red flags can look pretty orange in the right light. Be honest with yourself in the early stages of a relationship, and remember that you deserve love and support.

Try not to focus exclusively on a new partner's good points

It's tempting to file the bad ones away to deal with at a later date. You need to have your eyes wide open and look at all sides of a partner's personality right from day one.

It is incredibly easy to find yourself in an abusive relationship. It can be horribly embarrassing and make you feel ashamed that you have let certain things happen and you have allowed someone to treat you so badly. It can happen to anyone, and it's nothing to be ashamed of.

Feeling in the dark about what is actually happening can go on for a long time

You can continue to fool yourself that things will be better, or that it's normal to have such conflict. But the moment you recognise the reality of your situation, that can be the beginning of the end.

If you've never had a boyfriend before, your inexperience can be taken advantage of. I can tell you that being bullied by your partner is not the way it's meant to be. Every boy is not like it, this is not just how guys are. Keeping secrets from your friends and family is not a hallmark of an adult relationship, no matter what he might tell you.

Abusers are always going to apologise

And you are always going to want to accept it. If someone is apologising to you and they are very remorseful, it's hard not to forgive them and move on. You want it to be done, because no one wants this horribleness hanging over them. But when the situation happens again and again, they are not sorry. They just apologise to gaslight you.

Being treated like rubbish can be soul destroying because it can start to make you lose hold of who you are. Over time, the things they say impact your self-esteem. You start to believe you deserve less, because they make you feel worthless, and a downward spiral can start. As the weeks pass, you become used to the behaviour and you normalise it. That may be your normal, but it's not normal and you deserve more.

Culturally, as a woman, you are told that 'no one's perfect', 'every relationship has its ups and downs', 'you should be grateful that you have someone sticking by you' and 'the grass is always greener'. What we don't say is that sure, no one's perfect, but there are some serious personality flaws that no person should have to live with. The grass is actually greener outside of an abusive relationship, even if that means being alone.

A mature person takes responsibility for their actions

An abusive partner will often then turn the focus back on to you, reassigning the blame for their poor behaviour. 'It's because you make me feel a certain way that I treat you like trash.' You then do wonder, *Is this my fault? Am I this terrible person who deserves to be treated this way?* Absolutely not.

What to consider before having plastic surgery

We live in a culture of instant access, banks wanting to loan money, and the idea that everything is available at the click of a button. But we were both raised to be financially responsible. The ultimate rule that we abide by is: if you can't afford to buy it twice, you can't afford it.

PLASTIC SURGERY IS EXPENSIVE. Look at the priorities of your life. If all your goals are about buying a flat, don't spend a good percentage of your potential deposit on surgery.

SURGERY CAN GIVE YOU A BIG CONFIDENCE BOOST AND REDUCE ANXIETY AROUND CERTAIN ASPECTS OF YOUR APPEARANCE. It can make you feel like you walk taller and that a weight has been lifted from your shoulders.

SURGERY DOES CHANGE YOUR APPEARANCE. It does what it is supposed to do. If you are happy with your results it's like, *Wow, that is better*. And that is amazing. But the reality of that experience is that it can lead you down the path of, *Well, what's next?* Where else can you apply that magic? You can very easily get addicted to that surge of confidence.

SURGERY DOESN'T HARM ANYONE ELSE. It's your body, it's your decision. What anyone else thinks should not be a consideration.

SURGERY CANNOT FIX ALL OF THE PROBLEMS IN YOUR LIFE. A new nose or bigger lips will not get you a new job or a husband. It might give you more confidence, which might make achieving those goals more likely in the future, but it's no cure-all.

What to do if your friends don't like him

Without knowing the context, it would be very easy to say that if your friends don't like your boyfriend, it's a red flag. But the reality is that it all depends on what your relationship is like with your friends.

CONSIDER ALL ANGLES. If you step back, you may find that your 'friend' is trying to steer you in the wrong direction, and she is the toxic party.

WHAT IS IMPORTANT TO YOU? You have to ask yourself, how do you feel happy and supported?

LISTEN. If your friends are concerned about your relationship, they need to come to you with concrete examples of the behaviour that has caused this concern. Take in what they share, and consider the evidence.

WEIGH IT UP. It's important to get to the root of where the animosity is coming from. Is it something he's said? It can't just be like, *We don't really vibe with him.* That is not a thing.

BE OPEN AND CLEAR. We believe that an open conversation is the most important thing here. If this man is not going anywhere, and he is in your life, you need to find some common ground where you can all be civil.

FIND A SOLUTION IF YOU CAN! Suggest your friend spends some quality time with your boyfriend. If your friend and partner love you, they will come up with a solution to take the drama out of the situation.

The most important boy qualities

Kindness

Loyalty

Generosity of spirit (with their energy and time)

Affectionate

Confident and sure of himself

Ambitious with goals

Supportive, cheerleader

Sense of humour

Family-minded

Discretion

Mature

Respectful

CHAPTER FOUR

Single and Ready to Mingle

While there is so much focus on how to navigate relationships, we often say that there is not enough attention paid to single life – outside of the 'sad' Bridget Jones stereotypes. A lot about being single is about the relationship you develop with yourself, which we look at in more detail in the next chapter, but when you're newly single, perhaps just out of your first high school or uni relationship, it can be so hard to know how you're meant to meet people, what your boundaries should be – especially when you are still so relatively inexperienced – and of course, what you should be looking for out there. The world of dating is a lot and this is definitely a period of life that we get the most dilemmas about. Singledom is so fun, but it can involve *so many* ups and downs. But there is also so much joy to be found both on your own and with dating, even with the trials and tribulations. This chapter covers the period of our young-adult lives when we were both single at the same time – a time that we would agree was probably one of the best moments in both of our lives to date. We absolutely loved single life and if you are currently going through a break-up, or have been single for a while, we really wanted to share some of our experiences to make you feel less alone in it and, hopefully, make you feel excited to take that step into the next phase of your life.

Dilemma One

I broke up with my boyfriend of four years nearly six weeks ago and while I know it was the right decision and I'm not pining at all, I am starting to feel pressure from both friends and family to start dating – as if I won't be fully 'over' my ex until I 'get back out there'. Do you think they're right and should I stop dragging my feet?

S: Oh my gosh, this is such a thing and honestly, I do not know why! I'm sure it's all well meaning from your friends and family, but there is just absolutely no rush. You've just been with the same boy for four years, like, give yourself some breathing room! For both Cinz and me, we were so *so* sure that we did not want to be in a relationship – even a superficial one – for a long time after our break-ups.

C: We were in the mindset that we would be single for ages and ages. We were talking in *years*. We were saying our next boyfriends would be our husbands, because it was so far away. We just wanted to have *fully* alone time.

S: We didn't see boys on our radar for at least a year. Well, Cinzia was like, FIVE YEARS MINIMUM.

C: Soph, the reality is that my experience of males up to that point had been overall pretty shit. On top of my personal experience, we were also engaging with hundreds of dilemmas where guys were treating girls absolutely horrendously. Cheating, lying, disrespecting, you name it. So, we were like, *Men? No, thank you.*

S: Six weeks after my break-up, I wasn't thinking a single thought about boys or dating other people. Neither of us was speaking to anyone, or even a whiff of anything boy related. I was just so enjoying not having to carry anyone else's emotions and it felt like, *Wow, now I can have fun and get back to my old self* and you should absolutely feel like you can enjoy that moment without any kind of pressure to 'move on'.

C: Also, I think it's worth saying that there is always some kind of hangover from a break-up even if you walked away or it was entirely amicable. You need some space and time to rationalise it all and digest it emotionally. In my case, I had been thinking about breaking up with my ex for a long time and when you've been thinking about doing something for so long and then you do it, you realise what a toll it has been taking on you. These kinds of feelings can consume you. When it's been on your mind for months, if not years, when you finally make the decision and you're free of that situation, you feel like a new person.

S: That feeling of being free again is just the best . . . When it comes to our most recent experience, it was honestly like the stars had aligned for a hot girl summer, wasn't it?

C: It was so like that! Young, sexy and single. I think both of us had got to the point that we were so relieved to be on our own. Everything felt like a proper new chapter.

S: For us it was the best time ever – perhaps of our lives, to that date. I was on cloud nine every day! Timing-wise it all seemed to be perfect. The lockdown was over, we were spending more time in London and going out all the time.

C: We were also so excited because neither of us had been properly single as adults together. We were like, the world should brace itself!

S: The last time I'd been single, I'd just left school and I was working my part-time job. We had been building our channel, I wasn't sure what was going to happen with my future, and we didn't have a career. I was also living at home. And now, hello. I'm in my early twenties, I'm fortunate enough to be able to live on my own, I've built this amazing career that I love, and I remember feeling like I had so much more self-confidence. I really knew what I could bring to the table, and so much more about who I was and what I wanted than when I was younger. I one hundred per cent knew what I didn't want and how I didn't want to feel in a relationship. We were the absolute poster girls for singledom. Single life is the only life! You should be single for your whole twenties! Boyfriends are so irrelevant, they add nothing!

C: Boys come and go; you need to be so selfish!

S: I was so proud of us that we were so excited, content and happy to be alone. Because long-term break-ups can be so hard. Looking back, I feel like I went through all the heartbreak while I was still in my relationship – perhaps you feel something similar, which is why you're not pining. I often think we check out emotionally from relationships *way* before we physically leave. It's like you've played through every scenario to try to make it work every way you can think of, but then when you know it's over, it's over. I went through all that upset, turmoil and tears while I was still in it. So, when I came out of it, I wasn't crying, I wasn't upset, it just felt like freedom.

C: It's like you're almost mourning the relationship before you even leave it, when you realise it isn't for you. And you go through the break-up so many times in your mind, so that when you finally do it, you almost feel like you've already lived it. Of course, if you're the one who has been broken up with, things can be the absolute opposite and we know that heartbreaks can be *hard* because we have been on that side of the coin too. They say it can take you at least half the time you've been with a person to get over them – crazy, right? If you are going through that pain now, all we can say is we are sorry, but there is a light at the end of the tunnel and, one day, you will wake up and you won't feel so heartbroken, you'll actually start to feel like yourself again.

S: I think because we had been so emotionally drained by getting out of our relationships, we just had zero bandwidth for boys and that is so normal. No matter how the break-up happened, I think it's really important to take every single day that you need. People might want to encourage you to get right back into the dating scene, but if you're not ready, you could get really hurt, because not everyone out there is above taking advantage of your vulnerability. I remember us saying how empowering we found it that no one was texting us and we weren't getting these messages from strangers. We didn't have any male company and we couldn't have cared less. We didn't feel like there was any kind of void. I wasn't missing anyone and we weren't crying into our pillows.

C: When you have a boyfriend – or you're even just seeing someone enough to feel like you need to text them – you've got to keep in touch at some level. Let them know a bit about what you're doing, even if it isn't all day. And we just felt so free that we were on our own time, doing exactly what we wanted to do without, oh, I'd better message so-and-so, or what shall I text? There was a lot more headspace. I cannot recommend taking that pause more – there is just no rush, you're not going to 'miss' Mr Right just because you focus on yourself for a few weeks or months. You are the one calling the shots now, so only pay attention to your own schedule.

Dilemma Two

I've been single for ten months and I'm about ready to get out there and start dating again. But I have been out of the game for a long time – since I was fourteen and at school and I just don't know where to start! Any tips, greatly appreciated.

C: When I broke up with my ex, the only memories of being single that I had were being a kid. The only way I'd ever met a boy was in a club – and that's not dating. So, I was like, *Are we going to have to go back to snogging strangers in a club? Is that what it is?* Like what do we do?

S: Just like you, we were also like, *What is single life? How are we supposed to do it?* Do you go on a date every week? Do you date lots of different people at the same time? Where do you meet them? We were so clueless, because being single was so foreign to us. One of the things that really helped us was starting *The Single Files* on our podcast. The space that we had found as we came out of our relationships helped us refocus on work and it was like, right, let's sync up again and think about what we're going to do for the next year.

C: We decided to start the series exactly because we were both trying to navigate single life together with no real idea of what we were doing. We were both single, we were adults, we knew what we wanted, but also it just all seemed so overwhelming. It can be so difficult to know where to start, can't it?

S: So, we thought that having a little series would be a nice way to record all the new experiences we were going through and give a bit of structure to our single life. We also hoped it would be something that could really help other girls as well, as they learnt the single ropes, like what you're going through now. The podcast has always been focused on other people's problems, but now every fourth or fifth episodes would be about our dilemmas as we got to grips with being newly single.

While I was in my relationship, I had constantly been feeling like I needed to explore more of the world out there. I wanted to meet all sorts of different guys and speak to people who lived in different cities and had completely different perspectives on the world. I knew for sure that I needed to see so much more of what was out there so I would perhaps have a chance of having more in common with someone. I wanted to have different conversations and come into contact with different personalities, so I was up for dating well outside of my comfort zone, which I think is a really good headspace to be in.

C: When we first started *The Single Files*, we thought we were going to have this crazy year of single life and dating, and be able to go on trips and be meeting so many people. But then November 2020 hit, and we were like, *Oh God*. We've got this podcast talking about our crazy dating lives, and now we were on our sofas on a Friday night watching Netflix because of the lockdown. So, dating apps became the only option.

S: We'd actually downloaded them just before lockdown and put together our profiles. From July to the beginning of October, it was pure single life. There wasn't anyone knocking on our door, because we were putting out some pretty serious anti-boy energy. But then we started to feel ready to dip our toes back in. One of the best things about dating apps is that you can set them for any location, and we wanted to meet people from everywhere. It was at that point that we also realised we were ready to think about moving to London. While we absolutely love Nottingham, it had started to feel like it was time for some new experiences, and we needed a change of scene. As we were going to London most weekends outside of lockdown, it made sense to look there. Also, we thought, *What are the chances of meeting the perfect person in your home town?* In Nottingham everyone knows everyone, it's a very intertwined city. We wanted to meet people that came from a totally different place both geographically and in terms of their life experience.

Just seeing who was out there, matching with people, and having someone that likes you, is also such a confidence thing. It gives you that reassurance that you've still got it, you're still dateable, even if you're not entirely ready to date again. I would always recommend it to anyone like you who is slowly getting ready to put themselves back out there.

C: For us, we had no intention of finding boyfriends. We were just curious to meet different kinds of people and to just *date* as an exercise of personal growth in itself. We were definitely intrigued to see how different the whole boy thing would be because we were now really clear on what we wanted. Before we had been in our relationships, we both put up with all sorts and we weren't that picky when we were choosing. We were just thrilled that a boy liked us. So, we thought it would be interesting to meet someone and be able to see things from a position of more confidence. To be able to see the red flags and shut it down. Making those decisions is really important and, as a woman, being able to say, 'No, actually, you may be attractive, but I'm not interested,' even if a guy likes you, is as much of a rite of passage as losing your virginity.

S: Having virtual conversations on dating apps was a really good first step because it helped us build up our self-assurance with talking to someone new. From being in a long-term relationship to sitting on a date with a stranger is the biggest jump. And you ask yourself, *What do I say? How do I make this conversation interesting? What are we going to talk about?*

C: Making your profile is a lot of pressure, though. What can I say that's witty? Is this my best picture? What shall I say I do as my job? We also worried about catfishes and fake profiles. A girl's got to be careful in this day and age.

Just before we were totally locked down, we had both met two boys online and we had the chance to meet them for a physical date. We had been going down to London for dribs and drabs for work, and we thought, *Let's do it.*

S: I'd actually already organised a double date for us with this boy I was speaking to, but we had backed out of it the day of.

C: Oh my God, I forgot about that!

S: I had matched quite quickly with this guy, and he was very much in my comfort zone. He was similar in vibe and looks to my ex. It felt like a very easy hop and like I already knew him, which obviously hadn't been my plan, but there you go. Within our first conversation, he had asked me to go on a date. And I was like, sure. So, then I said to Cinzia, let's make it a double date. We were in London and by this point, I'd been speaking to this guy for a while, and it had quickly got to the point where he was FaceTiming me every single day.

C: All hours, as well. She'd be with me, and he'd be calling at two in the afternoon. Then again at 8 p.m.

S: I felt very comfortable, we had a lot to talk about, and it became a company thing. I was still speaking to plenty of other people, so I was never ensconced in it. The time finally came around for us to meet, a few weeks before the second lockdown closed in.

C: We basically just psyched ourselves out of it.

We didn't have any male company and we couldn't have cared less.

S: I think we got a bit nervous and we got cold feet. It was going to be our first date since our relationships, and we just lost our bottle. So, then we bailed and I remember thinking, *Well, that's it, isn't it? I'm never going to speak to that boy again, am I?* But somehow, we kept on speaking. Every single day. It was the type of communication you would have if you were in a relationship. So, the next time we were down in London, we arranged to meet – and at this point, it's days before lockdown.

C: And by this point I'd started speaking to this other boy. So, we both arranged to meet them for a walk in a park on exactly the same day, at exactly the same time. We left the hotel together at the same time: good luck, good luck, kiss, kiss. We were shitting ourselves.

S: We were overthinking every single step. Cinzia was like, 'When I get out of my taxi, what do I do? What if he can see me and I can't see him?'

C: I was obsessed that he was going to see my taxi pull up and would be watching me, but I wouldn't know where he was. I mean, who cares!? The things you get caught up with are crazy. But, anyway, it went well. There were a few moments when we were out walking together and I had this surreal feeling of guilt and fear and excitement, because I was out with another boy in a romantic scenario. I think it was the realisation of, *God, I'm not in that other relationship any more, this is a totally different person, and it's a totally different version of me too.* It felt really good. It was a clean slate, and I was getting to know this person for the first time, which felt fun and exciting and new.

S: I remember finding it so refreshing that we didn't know the same people at all. Anyone I knew, he didn't know, and he didn't know their cousin or a friend of a friend, either. There was no overlap, which again felt like a fresh start.

C: After that date, we managed to get one more in-person date that week. It was a dinner date, and that was both of our first proper dates out. For me, it was lovely and we kissed. And then we were locked down again (FFS!). But even back then, I had this really strong feeling that something was going to happen with him. You have to check yourself, and I definitely knew I had to hold my horses, but they do say, when you know, you know.

S: I remember feeling like, *uh oh*, at the time. Like, Cinz, remember you wanted to live your proper single life?! For five years, right? But let's not get ahead of ourselves. So, we both went on these dinner dates, and then we were back in lockdown. It was so frustrating, because we'd both met these boys we'd been speaking to and now, damn, we can't see each other again for who knows how long. We'd both had these lovely dates, and I'd kissed my boy too. I remember how weird kissing someone new had felt, but it was a good weird, in a way that I was ready to feel again. But obviously everything went on the back-burner.

During lockdown, we spoke to a lot of boys, but of course we couldn't feasibly meet up with them. I started doing a lot of FaceTime dates – it was like, F*uck it; I'll FaceTime you*. I was in my house by myself, so it was kind of fun and gave me something to do during the evenings. It was almost exactly like going on a date. I'd put some make-up on and a clean top, do my hair and FaceTime this boy. You'd both have a drink and it was the closest thing you could do to a date. I remember the whole process feeling like I was gaining even more conviction in my own confidence, and I did really enjoy it. Being about to call someone you don't know and hold a conversation, I remember being like, *Wow, I don't know if I'd have been able to do that before*. This is a life skill. Obviously, I would rather have been able to physically date all these people, but we had to roll with the circumstances, so I would absolutely say give online dating a shot, because it is such a good way to get back out there and gain some confidence.

Dilemma Three

I've been dating a lot of guys over the past year, and I have had some really depressing experiences where I've been ghosted or just let down over time. I wondered if you guys had ever been through anything like that and how did you cope?

S: I think every single girl who has ever dated has had similar experiences to you and it can be absolutely crushing. I went through a similar thing with the guy that I was FaceTiming – that boy I went on those two real-life dates with. We spoke every bloody day through the lockdown, but there was just no sense of progress of any kind. When the lockdown lifted, I understandably presumed that as we'd been talking for so long and we had already kissed, perhaps on my next trip to London we could see where it was going to go. We were now in March. I hadn't seen this boy since November, and we were still speaking. Every. Single. Day. It'd been months, but looking back, I probably should have seen a signal in the fact that he hadn't made one move to try to plan anything or to organise seeing me for when we were allowed to. Several times, I had tried to suggest things we could do together after the lockdown ended, but he never seemed to want to commit to anything. But I never really thought that he didn't like me, because the boy was calling me three times a day! He wanted to talk to me constantly, and we didn't speak about the idea of talking to other girls or boys.

I was absolutely still on the dating apps and I was talking to other people, because I still wasn't in the right place to entertain a relationship, even though over the months it had started to feel more like boyfriend–girlfriend because of the sheer amount of time we spent speaking. In lots of ways, I did think it was a good thing that we had that time to build a conversational relationship rather than being in physical contact all the time, but still it gets to a point with every person that you meet on a dating app when something is either going to become more of a thing, or it's not. It wasn't a friendship app after all.

C: It all came to a head when we got to London. We had decided to rent a flat for a whole month because we had a lot of work on and we really wanted to feel a little more settled when we were in London and get our bearings better than we could staying in a hotel. We each brought two huge suitcases and we were ready to go!

S: I had just presumed that as soon as I got there, I'd be going on dates with this boy, I'd be able to see him in person and we would hang out. I didn't know where it was going to go, but I was sure there was some kind of journey about to start. But for some unfathomable reason, every time we spoke he wasn't asking me to hang out and when I asked, he would say, 'I'm busy today, I can't make it work.' There are only so many times you can ask a boy – even one you have been speaking to every day for months – to make a plan. What the hell was going on?

C: He was only fifteen minutes down the road! Whenever he came up on FaceTime, I'd say, 'Come see us, come see Sophia, come see our place, it's just around the corner!' We'd been in London for two weeks by then, and it was just excuse after excuse.

S: It was such a confusing experience. It ended up getting to the end of this month, and it was like, *We're going home next week. WTF.* I remember at that point feeling so deflated and that last week in London was really hard. Don't get me wrong, it wasn't like I was sitting around waiting for the phone to ring. I actually went on lots of other dates with a bunch of interesting people. There was a record producer and a guy who worked in fashion, and generally it had been a great experience. But there hadn't been any chemistry with any of them and there was just no sense that I wanted to see them again.

C: I remember you coming home every time and saying, 'Do you think I should go on a second date?' I think if you have to ask that question, the spark isn't there.

S: I'd gone on all these dates with different people, I wasn't really clicking with anyone, but there's this great guy that I have been speaking to for six months, fifteen minutes down the road, but he doesn't want to see me? But he *still* keeps calling? Since November! I'll say it again, it wasn't like I wanted him to be my boyfriend, because I still wasn't there at all. But I did want to spend time with him, as we had connected, and the whole thing boggled my mind because I cared about him, and I thought he cared about me.

Finally, I said to him, 'Are you busy on Friday, because I'm going home on Saturday?' And all of a sudden, he had this urgency to see me, so I was like, 'OK, let's go for a walk. Or come round and we can order something.' And then a couple of hours before we went on the walk, he messaged me: 'Just before we meet, I just want to let you know that, for me, this is a friendship and I value you so much as a friend.' I remember reading it and I was like, *What?*

Regroup, take a breath and realise that no one who is right for you will pass you by.

C: He said, 'I don't want to lead you on.' I was stunned, like, *What is he talking about?* Soph and I had to go back to the flat to have a little sit-down. At no point in the hundreds of hours he had been talking to Sophia had he been clear. He was constantly present and the signals, at least until we'd come to London, had all pointed towards him being into it.

S: I replied, basically saying, 'Is this you friend-zoning me?' And he was like, 'Don't put it like that.' He then made the point that we'd never spoken about our feelings or ever known where we stood. And that was true; we'd never mentioned what we wanted or what we were looking for or anything like that. I'd never put him on the spot, but I think that was because it had felt romantic at the beginning, so I hadn't really thought to *define* it afterwards. In retrospect, I suppose it might also have been because I knew somewhere that something was off.

C: I just couldn't believe it.

S: I remember feeling so stupid. After that, the penny dropped. Of course, he wasn't interested in me, because if he had been, he would have seen me. He hadn't been busy; he'd been avoiding me for a month. All that confidence I'd gone into this new chapter of dating with, just dissolved. I felt like I was totally clueless. He insisted on seeing me before I went home, so he finally came round, and I was finally seeing this boy again. Not quite as I'd imagined, but anyway.

C: I was hiding in the other room!

S: It ended up being a really emotional conversation. He was really upset, which seemed unusual considering he was talking to someone he didn't want to be involved with and he was the one rejecting me. It was all, 'There's no girl like you, no one's like you. We're so close. I value you so much as a friend.' The ultimate point he was trying to make was that we had become such close friends, he was worried that if it went to a romantic place, we'd lose our friendship.

C: But isn't that the perfect foundation for a beautiful relationship?

S: Right! So, I was like, 'Let's dial this back. I wasn't even looking for a boyfriend, so, you've made that up yourself.' I just thought I was going to get to London, we'd hang out in person, build on this relationship that we'd already established, and see what happened. There was no pressure. I was not pursuing him; I wasn't chasing him down. I just thought we got along really well, so who knows?

The nail in the coffin was when I asked him exactly what it was he wanted, and he said that he wanted it to keep going just as it was. Speaking every single day, all day long, just not in a romantic way.

C: We also knew that as soon as he knew that Sophia was dating someone else, or had a new boyfriend, he would freak out, because that level of intensity is not normal in a friendship. Right then, the whole thing was easy for him, because they could be these best mates and there was no one else on the scene. But it was never going to be like that for ever.

S: Anyway, that was a sad load of rejection. It clearly didn't go the way I had seen it going, and it all came from out of the blue for me. I had thought that all the signs pointed to him liking me, he *told* me that he liked me, but he didn't. I felt like I'd wasted my time, and of course it hurt. When I got back home, I remember thinking, *Right, well, I can't speak to you after that debacle.* And I did feel sad about that and missed him. No messages, no calls, no one on the cards, back to square one. Occasionally, we would still speak as 'friends', but it was like once we had decided we were going to be friends, we weren't any more at all. Being let down by someone that you feel you have a connection with is gutting, but you have to just regroup, take a breath and remember that no one who is right for you will pass you by.

Dilemma Four

I've been dating on and off for the past couple of months and I haven't yet met someone I connect with. I know you two now have new boyfriends – how did you know that they were worth investing more of your time? Did you know it straight away or was it more of a third-date thing?

C: I suppose I could say in my heart of hearts I did kind of know as soon as I met my current boyfriend that he was special. While I did speak to other boys, I just couldn't switch off from him. I definitely wasn't thinking about it in relationship terms, because there was just this sense during lockdown that any romantic connection wasn't really real. It wasn't a real-life relationship, so why spend any time worrying about it? It was like playing with Monopoly money and we were just having a nice time together. Soph and I were still doing *The Single Files* – and there's only so much you can gauge, anyway, from just talking to someone on the phone – so I made no commitments at all and just enjoyed it. Over time, I definitely felt it edging into boyfriend territory, but neither of us discussed what would happen after lockdown. He wasn't stupid and he had female friends who listened to the podcast, and people had obviously been relaying things that we were saying. He actually told me that he thought he'd never see me again as soon as lockdown was over. A lot of times, he thought that I was just going to put it off the minute real life started back up – and I have to admit, I was in two minds.

My gosh, how many relationships out there must have been the same? During lockdown, with anything even semi-new, you just had no idea how it would really play out in real life. We hadn't been in normal life with each other, so what were we? We'd only been on two dates, but because we'd spoken so much and got to know each other so well, did that mean we were further along than just two dates? I'd have conversations with Sophia and my sister, because by this point my feelings were involved. I'd be like, I can't just break it off without giving it a bit of a go, even though I'd had no intention of being anyone's girlfriend. It kind of crept up on me. I mean, I was committed to dating, but the circumstances really derailed the whole plan.

S: I remember thinking at the time, because I wasn't in it and I could see it from afar, that it was a shame you hadn't had the chance to live your single life before you were back in something else again. Obviously, I didn't know him, because I didn't have the chance to get to know him, but as soon as I could see there were feelings involved, I did think that. Like, there was a gap in terms of time, because you'd been single for months. But in terms of what you'd been able to experience in the in-between, it had been so impacted by the pandemic.

C: That was a constant thought for me too. Because I had been stuck in not so great relationships in the past, I didn't want to just find myself in something not right again.

S: I remember, at the time, thinking that you had been cheated of that single-time experience. But look, that's sometimes just how life is. It laughs at your plans!

C: One moment I was going to be out every night, I was going to be single for five years, it was going to be total carnage. And then suddenly, I blinked, and this boy was in my life. On the last weekend of lockdown, Soph and I had made a plan and rented a flat in London. My boy was shitting himself thinking, that's it, she's moving to London, and she's had enough of me. We ended up having a few emotional conversations and, in the end, we just agreed to take it day by day. Let's see what it's like when we can actually date, when we can actually talk to each other in the context of our real lives, our jobs, our families, our friends. Let's see what happens when this bubble bursts. We hadn't even been to a bar together yet, for God's sake! I wanted us to play catch-up and experience all of the things that we should have been doing months before. And we did that, and it was wonderful, and in real life he was just as good as he'd been on the screen. I just realised I'd got in too deep, and despite my best-laid plans, it looked like I was *not* going to be single for the next five years.

S: For me, I will definitely say there was an instant spark that felt so different from all the other dates I'd been on. The same night that I'd been pied off by the FaceTime boy, I'd logged back on to Hinge – obviously to soothe my fragile ego. It was still our hot girl summer, and I was still seeking those experiences and connections. I just tried to put it into perspective and remind myself that my feelings might be slightly bruised, but it was all part of the experience. That very night, I matched with this other boy and I remember thinking, *Aw, he's quite cute.*

I started speaking to him briefly and then he gave me his number. I wasn't really interested at all, and when I woke up the next morning I felt like I needed a total break from boys again. I didn't feel like I wanted to go on any dates, I didn't want to get

Despite my best-laid plans, it looked like I was not going to be single for the next five years.

upset again. I had an appointment at my hairdresser's, and she started to ask me about my love life and I just said, 'Nothing – no dates, nothing to report.' Then just off the cuff, I mentioned that I *did* have this one guy's number. And she was like, 'Go on. Just message him, what have you got to lose?' I was like, 'No, I can't be arsed! For what?! They just mess you up.' Anyway, over the two hours in foils, she ended up convincing me to WhatsApp him, and he replied immediately. I remember thinking, *Whoa, this boy is keen.*

Very quickly, things felt different. Within a few messages, he said, 'I'd love to see you at the weekend, what are you doing on Friday?' I replied, 'I'm busy on Friday,' and I didn't offer any sort of other option. But then he came back and said, 'What about Sunday?' Sure, yeah, OK, Sunday. After that, I didn't speak to him for the rest of the week, and the whole I-can't-be-bothered energy came back. I felt like I didn't want to invest any more time into anyone before I knew they liked me; I wanted to make sure that we had a connection. Fuck having another friend on FaceTime.

C: The night before Soph's date, we were out in London in a club. We were a bit drunk . . . OK, I was quite drunk. Let's say it was messy. And Soph was like, 'I'm not going on this date tomorrow.' I can remember forcibly telling her, 'You will. You will wake up, have breakfast, wash your hair and go.'

S: For some reason, I FaceTimed him from the club. I mean. Not what we would advise anyone to do, probably. But at least I knew he was who he said he was. The next day I was just so anti the idea of going on the date. I think I was still wrapped up in that post-rejection negativity and thinking that the dates I'd been on hadn't led to anything, and I was getting fed up of going out with people whom I didn't really fancy. I just thought, *Fuck this, I just want to be by myself.* I was in a negative dating place; I didn't want another shit date with someone I didn't fancy, with the whole bruised feelings in the background. I wasn't sure my ego could take it.

C: I remember you standing there, with your bag on your shoulder, saying I'M NOT GOING. She had her shoes on, but was still saying I'M NOT GOING. And me and my boyfriend, who was over then, were like, 'You're going, *just go!*' She ended up storming out of the door shouting, 'I DON'T WANT TO DO THIS!'

S: Like a mardy teenager!

C: Then as soon as she got in his car, she sends a picture. And she's all happy.

S: I was in my trackie top, wearing leggings I'd worn in bed, hungover, and I hadn't washed my hair. And the minute I saw him, I was like, *Fuck. I should have at least put my jeans on.* Off the back of my FaceTime friend, where there were no plans, it was a big surprise to find someone who made an effort. He came to pick me up, walked me to his car, and then said that he'd organised this whole itinerary. He was going to take me to a place in west London that he thought I'd really like, and then for a little drive. We had a really nice first date and I felt instinctively that there was something there. I knew I actually liked him, I had butterflies and I was sure that I wanted to see him again. We had really good conversations; he seemed layered and like he knew who he was – it just felt really different from every other date I'd been on. It was also a totally sober date, just getting to know each other. Midway through the first date we agreed to the second one, then I gave him a little fist bump at the end and got out of the car, and that was it.

C: The rest is history. You didn't ever once question if you wanted to see him again. You just knew.

S: A couple of days later, he messaged to say that for the next date on the Friday night he'd booked a table for eight o'clock at his favourite Italian, and that he would be coming to pick me up. And I was like, *Ohhhhh, this is how it's supposed to be.* This is how you know they want to see you . . . because they make bookings. They tell you before. They let you know. It was such a stark contrast. But this is the energy they should bring. And then on the Friday, he would say, 'Can we do breakfast on Sunday?' Every single weekend went that way, from the very first date, and here we are.

What we've learnt is that you shouldn't have to ask the question, 'What are we?' If someone likes you, and if someone is interested, you will know exactly what you are, or at least where it's headed. If you like them and you are interested, you won't have to question anything. You won't be confused and you won't be doubting yourself.

C: You're not holding anything back, they're not holding anything back. You just know.

S: I think the most important takeaway from that experience is that if my FaceTime friend hadn't dropped me that night, and if I had tried to cling on to that non-relationship, I would never have matched with my now-boyfriend. I went on Hinge because I was feeling rejected, and I probably would never have replied to him if I hadn't been so down. I don't believe that during your dating journey you meet your true love when everything is perfect. I was hurt, a bit wobbly and wearing bed leggings. It did not bode well. You cannot predict when on earth you will bump into someone who is going to change your life – it is all a game of chance. Equally, you can't date and be sure that you aren't going to find your boyfriend week one, date one.

As hurtful as it can be, you have to see rejection as protection. It's such a big sign from the universe, that this boy is not the one and the real one is probably just around the corner. While it can be tempting to try to change their mind, and continue investing your time and heart into someone you care so much for, it will never end well. If someone rejects you, let them reject you, because they are actually doing you a favour and pointing you in a new and better direction.

What we do know is that there should be no confusion. The fact that I was so muddled in both my relationship with my ex and my FaceTime friend was the red flag. In both instances, that confusion should have been enough for me to say hello, there's obviously something not right here, but in both situations, I made excuses and tried to avoid confronting it.

C: If a guy wants you to be his girlfriend, he will ask you to be his girlfriend. If he's trying to avoid it, he doesn't. If you aren't sure if you want to see a guy again or if you still want to be his girlfriend, then you probably don't. Communication with yourself, and then with the other person, is so incredibly important. You should never feel scared to have honest conversations, even if feelings might be hurt. It's not easy, but it is the *only* way.

First-date rules

- **IF THEY ASK, THEY SHOULD ARRANGE.** When it comes to a first date, we always believe that whoever does the asking should do the organising. If a guy messages on the day to say, 'So, where shall we go then?', for us, it shows a lack of decision and consideration. And this is the *first* date, imagine what it would be like if you were in a relationship.

- **YOU SHOULD ALWAYS OFFER TO SPLIT THE BILL.** You are offering with an intent to pay; your hand needs to be in your bag. If they insist on paying, make sure that on the second date, or perhaps at drinks after, you cover the bill. A date shouldn't be an opportunity to get a free meal.

- **BE SAFE AND CONSIDER DIFFERENT DATE OPTIONS.** If you are anxious about meeting someone and you're not sure that you want to spend too much time with them, a brief coffee can be great. We absolutely suggest a FaceTime call first if it will make you feel more comfortable.

● **DATES DON'T HAVE TO BE IN A BAR OR RESTAURANT.**
While it's easier to get a bit tipsy on a first date to take
away the nerves, alcohol can cloud the connection
and have an impact on your decision-making. If you're
really trying to get to know someone, being sober is the
best option.

Some good ideas for non-drinking dates include:
- bowling
- mini golf
- a museum or gallery trip
- a walk
- a pre-dinner coffee

A bad idea for a date: the cinema.
Avoid at all costs – you can't talk, you're physically
awkwardly close, and the experience will generally
be uncomfortable.

Before, during and after the date

● If you're meeting someone and you're nervous, start with a compliment. 'You smell great.' 'Love your jacket.' And then hopefully he'll give you one in return.

● Remember, it isn't just your job to carry the conversation. It's not as if you're going to be sitting talking to a wall, they equally want to have a conversation. Hopefully, within fifteen minutes you'll have a lovely flow, but moments of brief silence are normal.

● Don't talk about your ex. We don't mean that in the abstract, because often you'll be asked, or you'll ask, about when the last relationship ended, and so on. But do not get drawn into details. Don't bitch about your ex, and don't give a blow-by-blow rundown of how and why you broke up.

● If a guy doesn't ask you to text him when you get home, that's a red flag. It means he isn't considering your safety.

● The follow-up text should come immediately afterwards. Within ten minutes. If you leave the establishment, they should always make sure you get home, because that is a good sign they are a kind person.

- We would also expect the next date to be arranged, if it's going to happen, on the first date or immediately after – unless they are going on holiday or are in a job that doesn't allow for that, of course!

- These all mean they don't want to see you again:

I had a great time, hopefully see you around one of these days.

Would be great to bump into each other.

We should do this again sometime.

How to tell that he's just not that into you

If you are ever unsure if a guy is into you, that generally means he is not.

Hot and cold, mixed messages mean he's keeping you as an option on his roster, in case he can't find anything else.

If you are experiencing any of these, he's just not that into you:

- lack of effort
- the texting starts to taper off
- plans are not being made
- plans are being cancelled
- not keeping the conversation going
- he's on his phone on dates
- he's not asking questions
- he's not engaged with you
- he doesn't make eye contact

Dating red flags

Lateness (without a valid reason)

Rudeness to staff

Last-minute cancellations

Doesn't compliment you

Doesn't ask you questions

Tries to get
you drunk

No effort with
appearance

Expects you
to pay

Phone on table

Horrible to
everyone
but you

Is this dating profile legit?

Beware of minimal pictures (perhaps only one or two).

If you can't find them on Instagram or Facebook, be wary.

Avoid aggressive dating profiles like the plague.

Ask to FaceTime to make sure they are who they say they are.

Meet in a public place. Never go to their home on a first date, and make sure your friends or family know where you are going.

Feel free to stalk their digital profiles – tagged pics, mates. That is not psychotic behaviour, it's just smart.

How to communicate that you're not interested

Some guys can misinterpret you ignoring them – or 'ghosting' – as playing hard to get. *She's just playing a bit of a game*, they might think. So, save everyone the time and nip it in the bud right away. Copy and paste the below and use as required:

> I had a lovely time, but I don't see this going anywhere right now. It was so lovely to meet you, and I wish you all the best.

It takes two minutes, and then it's done.

Should you ever sleep with someone on the first date?

- Never say never.

- There are no right or wrong moves on the first date.

- Sex can be a great gauge of intimacy and compatibility.

- If the vibe is there, the vibe is there.

- Trust your instincts.

- Don't feel guilty for the experience if it was fun.

- Be safe and careful.

- As long as it was positive, don't overthink it.

- Sex can't offer you validation.

- Repeated one-night stands will eat away at your self-esteem, as constant meaningless contact with someone who doesn't care about you can grind your confidence down.

- Protect your heart, but do what feels right for you.

Dos and don'ts for the perfect dating profile

Do

Try to showcase a lovely mix of your personality.

Show your fun side, your traveller side, your sexy side, your friendship side.

Consider a dog pic. Dogs say, *I'm wholesome, I'm loyal, I like animals*.

A dating profile should reflect your lifestyle as well as your goals.

Be clear about what you're on there for, don't waste your time.

Keep your descriptions short and sweet.

Don't

Don't post the same selfie four times.

Don't look too Instagramy – 6 #OOTDs on your own pouting looks a little self-centred.

No gym selfies.

When it comes to the words, don't overthink it, feel free to experiment and switch it up.

CHAPTER FIVE

The Most Important Relationship of All

Whenever anyone talks about relationships, they're generally chatting about the dynamics you have with other people, but the first relationship and the one that influences every single other relationship that you have *throughout your life*, is the one you have with yourself. We always say that it isn't taken seriously enough, because if you want a positive and happy life, free from toxic relationships, full of great friends, and to be able to build a fulfilling career, you have got to get to know how you feel about yourself and what you want out of your life sorted first.

Not that we're saying that this is something that is easy or that we have ticked off our list. Your relationship with yourself is constantly evolving, and we know we still have so much to learn about ourselves as we gain more life experience. But we can definitely speak to that moment when you hit adulthood and how insecurities and naïvety can lead you down some negative paths with your self-esteem, which in turn can lead to you letting people into your life who either aren't right for you or don't deserve to be there. And we really wanted to share some of the ways that we have connected with ourselves, protected ourselves and made changes to our lives, to stay true to ourselves in both our professional and personal lives.

Dilemma One

I feel like I'm stuck in a massive rut in nearly every aspect of my life. Nothing is turning out how I hoped it would – I worked so hard in school and now I've worked hard to get my first job, but everything feels so underwhelming, and I feel like I'm not really excited about anything. It's like I need to upgrade my whole life but I have no idea how to go about it. I was just wondering how you managed to build such an amazing career and achieve so many of your goals.

C: To begin with this one, I think it's so important to remember that we live in a world where expectations are really, really high and that can sometimes make reality feel much tougher than what you might have envisaged when you left school. Everyone goes through that no matter what they decide to do for their career. But not feeling excited about anything that you are doing in life is something to be concerned about for sure. You haven't mentioned what it is that you imagined yourself doing, and perhaps that's because you don't really know, or you haven't really admitted it to yourself yet? We have always believed in the power of manifestation and talking to and about yourself with positivity to set you on a course towards the things that will fulfill you in life and it could be something that could help you work on your goals too.

S: We were definitely manifesting before we even knew what manifestation was. Like, I don't think we'd heard the word.

C: I remember when we used to watch jennxpenn and Lauren Elizabeth on YouTube when we were maybe fifteen, and one of Jenn's videos introduced us to the idea of writing letters to ourselves. In one video, she had written herself a letter a couple of years before and then, on her eighteenth birthday, she opened it and read it. The letter was full of all the things she had hoped to achieve and what she wanted to do. For us, that's where a lot of our manifestation started, because that was the beginning of us learning to articulate our goals and making plans for how we were going to achieve them. I remember we both wrote ourselves a letter when we were sixteen, to open on our eighteenth birthdays, and from that point, we did the same at the end of every year.

S: We truly believe we owe a lot to manifestation for everything that we have achieved in both our careers and private lives. There is a lot of skepticism out there, but for working out what it is you really do want, manifestation can be so valuable, so I would always say to people to keep an open mind.

There are lots of ways to manifest, from making vision boards to speaking our daily mantras, but most often we write lists of our goals and things we want to achieve. It can be personal, it can be about your emotions, it can be professional. Then we regularly refer back to the lists, so what we've written down stays front of mind. You need to constantly remind yourself and realign your mind towards your priorities and goals in your subconscious, until it becomes so naturally embedded in your mind, that every choice and action you make occurs in the context of furthering your goals.

What we know for sure is that you always see what you're focusing on in life. If you think about a yellow car, you will see yellow cars all the time. Equally, if you think positive things and good things about yourself, that's what you will see and feel. Conversely, if you're always thinking negatively, your whole world will become increasingly heavy. No one is going to make you have a good day – however hard it is, you are the only one who can control your reactions to the good and bad things that happen to us all on a daily basis. That's easier said than done of course. It takes practice and perseverance, to keep grateful when you're having an absolute shitshow of a day, but you really can turn your perception of things around.

When that happens, or when you achieve anything that you have previously manifested, or even just nailed one of the stepping stones along the way, you have to stop and celebrate. You have to observe the small victories. You also must keep looking around you and reminding yourself of how many positives there are already in your life, while you're still on the journey to your goals. There are times when things can feel really hard and like everything is going wrong and yes, you might feel lonely at some points, but you have to dig deep to find things to feel grateful about, because there is always something.

C: When it comes to manifesting your goals, I do think you have got to truly, wholeheartedly believe that something is going to happen, or it won't.

S: We have always backed ourselves when there was no real way of knowing if things were going to work out or not, which was probably more our naïvety than anything. But we've always clung on to that positive state of mind, especially when it comes to our careers.

C: We constantly say it *is* going to happen. Even if I had an inkling of private doubt, I'd always say to Sophia, 'Oh, no, no, no, this *is* going to work out.' Then she'd be like, 'You're right, it's fine.' And when we both believe something is going to be fine, most often it does turn out to be at least OK.

S: The thing about manifesting your goals is that they can be literally worlds away from where you are at that point in your life, so they *can* seem entirely unrealistic from where you are standing on day zero. So, while we know and think about our big goals, the absolute dreams that we want to achieve, we would say the most important part of the manifestation process is breaking down those topline goals into the steps that you will need to take to get there. It's mapping out how you're going to try to jump onto each of those stepping stones over the course of weeks, months and maybe even years. We drill it down to goals for today, goals for the week, goals for the month and so on, all of them driving towards the same final outcome – but on a more practical and manageable level.

C: I think that manifestation has a bad rep because most people seem to think it's just: say you want to do *this* and poof! It happens. But actually, it's all about doing the work *while* keeping these clear, focused goals in mind, all the way along the journey. You can't just sit on your sofa and say, 'I'm going to have this big empire' and this and that, and not do anything about it. Manifestation is a structure for you to change your life, it's not magic.

S: You have to have those realistic baby steps because, Jesus Christ, how else are you going to get there?
We've always had a strong work ethic, and if you want your manifestation to come to fruition, you do have to put the hours in. Even when we were doing A-levels and we had so much homework, every single weekend we would make the time to create our content because that was our passion. At the time, we had some followers, maybe a thousand people dipping in and out, but there wasn't a real sense of any kind of momentum or any suggestion that it was going to build to be anything like the platform we have today. We could have so easily thought, well, no one's really

Remember
we live in a
world where
expectations
are really
high

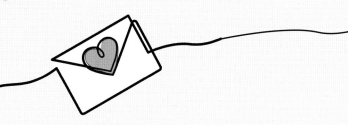

which can
make our
realities
feel tough.

watching, so who cares? But we always cared about it and that's why we kept posting.

Looking back, I do think that ballet had a really big influence on our characters when we were younger and made us focused.

C: Yeah. At the time, we weren't thinking about building a sense of self-discipline or anything like that. We were just dancing and having a laugh. Well, sometimes when we could get away with it. But when you look back, it was very strict, very regimented, and it wasn't always fun.

S: Some of our classes finished at 10 p.m., and we were going three times a week, even though we had a heavy homework load, and then we were up at 6 a.m. to get to school every morning. I'll never forget that feeling of getting home, shattered from school, and forcing myself to put on that leotard and go back outside on a freezing-cold, dark winter's evening. I don't think, as kids, you give yourself credit for those kinds of things. But in retrospect, I do think it was what gave us the foundations of discipline and helped build our drive. Ballet also definitely helped us to be extremely organised with our workloads and that has been a huge help when it's come to building our careers. If you had ballet, you couldn't leave your coursework to the last minute, you had to fit it all in somewhere. You just didn't have the chance to procrastinate. That attitude was what we took on to the blog and everything else we've done since. You can't just leave things to tomorrow, and you have to try to be good at time management, or else you won't be able to achieve what you set out to do.

C: Ballet was also a great lesson for me at least, in anchoring your goals within the realms of what is actually possible – it's all very well to say, manifest whatever you want, but there are some limits and I think it's really important to be honest about that. In those early years, I went to ballet because I seriously wanted to be a ballerina. When I was really young, I wanted to go to the Royal Ballet School, and I managed to get myself an audition – at the time, you had to send in pictures of yourself in positions. I had some level of talent when I was younger and I went to the audition with one other girl in our class, who was the top dog. She was so bouncy and literally born to be a dancer. We went down to Birmingham for this big audition, and it was extremely formal, intense and intimidating. The other girl got into the Royal Ballet and has since become a professional dancer, but I didn't. I still carried on with my classes and went to summer dance schools, but after that rejection . . . I mean, when you don't get into the Royal Ballet School, you *know*. There are so many goals where you can bend the world to your will, but when you're talking about raw talent, or your genetic abilities, there are also limits, and I think that ballet really taught me that, early on. We could sit here and say you can be anything you want to be, but if you can't sing in tune, you're probably not going to be the next Ariana.

There were lots of things we did through ballet that were really scary at the time. In my opinion, some of the intimidation was often slightly unnecessary, but our hobby really stretched and challenged us when we were children and I think that has had a huge impact in our adult lives, setting us up for the future.

S: I think the most important thing to say is that, on top of our relentlessly positive attitudes and true self-belief that we could build an amazing career outside of the usual avenues that school and our peers told us we had to walk down, we have always been dedicated and hard-working girls. We have always had a really strong work ethic, and learnt early that there are very few ways that you can reach any kind of success without that, no matter what it might look like from the outside. The fact that you have worked so hard to get to where you are *today* is something to congratulate yourself on and find gratitude in. Now all you need to do is refocus towards the next step and get directing all that effort towards something that will make you feel more satisfied and excited. Try not to lean into any feelings of disappointment or regret, there is just no point to waste your energy there – you are on your journey already, you've just come to that moment to find the next stepping stone.

Dilemma Two

I broke up with my long-term boyfriend about a year ago, because I felt like I was just going through the motions, and recently I've felt myself drifting away from my group of friends whom I have known since school. I feel guilty that I'm maybe growing out of my friendship group and I'm also scared that if I properly walk away, I won't make any new friends. I don't love doing things on my own, but I'm starting to feel like I just hang out with my friends because they are there. What should I do?

S: I think that you have to start by taking a bit of a long, hard look in the mirror. What is it that you want out of your relationships and what is it that you feel is missing from your current ones? Working out what you need from relationships can take a long time to process. Part of that is getting to know yourself – how can you decide on the right boyfriend or close friend for you when you don't even know who you are? As our confidence has grown, the women we have become have changed. I think there is such a resistance to that in our culture, this idea that by changing and evolving you have somehow betrayed people. No. We all mature and grow up and learn more about ourselves, and that should be supported rather than criticised. As much as feelings may be bruised, you can't stand still when you're not feeling fulfilled because you're scared that people around you won't support your growth. While it's easy to say, 'Just go and find new friends,' I would absolutely also say that it's worth seriously considering whether you really want to leave good people behind totally just because they don't perfectly fit into your life this second. Cinzia and I would always say don't jump to extremes – it might end up that you do have to close some doors, but that isn't something you have to decide on immediately. You can absolutely explore making new friends while trying to find new ways to connect with your old friends on terms that suit you better.

As for finding those people who meet your needs in life (both with boys and platonic friends), manifestation has also played a big part in our personal lives too.

C: For us, it starts with writing down the qualities that you want in a partner and relationships. Perhaps you've just got out of a bad relationship, and you feel like you can't go through that kind of experience again. So, you write down very clearly what you want, what you feel you deserve and how you want to be treated by a partner in the future. Having those words there – I often write mine on my iPhone notes, or in *The Girls' Bathroom: The Journal* so I can flick to them whenever I need to reaffirm my thoughts – I do believe that works, because then you are focused on only allowing that into your life. You will be less likely to accept poor treatment, and you notice it as soon as it's happening. When you meet new people, you can refer back to the list and be clear on your boundaries; then you will hopefully end up in a relationship or friendship with someone who has the majority of those traits.

Another major key to bringing the right people into your life is getting used to your own company and feeling totally comfortable on your own. Alone time is really important to centre yourself and to clear your mind. If you're always around other people, the noise can stop you hearing your inner voice, so it is really valuable to start practising spending time alone. When I get overwhelmed and sad, I just need to be on my own for a full twenty-four hours.

S: Same!

C: I just need to be in bed, literally not speak to anyone, and then I'm like, I'm OK, I'm kind of recharged and ready to face the world again. That's how I cope.

S: Alone time helps me too. I also always like to write my thoughts down and pinpoint exactly why I'm feeling the way I am. I think it's really valuable to look back at what has set those feelings in motion. We do overthink things sometimes, and experience doubt and dread. So, you have to work to calm those thoughts and voices and bring yourself back to positivity.

Sitting alone with your thoughts and being your own best company is something that takes time to get used to, but it *is* something you can learn to do. If you're trying to enjoy alone time, I think it always helps if you make sure your space is clean. It's so much nicer to relax in a clean space in contrast to a chaotic space. Clothes are put away, you light a candle.

C: Or your bedsheets are freshly washed and put on. Even just that one small thing. You deserve this, so treat yourself nicely.

Alone time is really important to centre yourself and clear your mind.

S: It's not like you're supposed to sit there in darkness, 'Right, I've got to learn to do this "alone time" thing.' It's meant to feel lovely. So, put your favourite show on, get some snacks, make a hot chocolate. Do things like you would with a girlfriend at a sleepover, but just do them on your own.

C: I love alone time because I can watch all the videos that I want to watch. Sophia doesn't like my videos, and I don't ever want to watch hers either. There's nothing better than being alone and getting to enjoy one hundred per cent exactly what you want to do. It does sometimes take time to learn what that is. Perhaps, if you're in a big friendship group, you may be a bit disconnected from what it is you actually like to do with your time. It can be easy to think you like something just because everyone else does. So, spending time on your own is a great space to explore that, and it can help you learn what makes you happy just for you. If that's making a meal that no one else likes – then so be it. Because until you know yourself, how can you ever understand what you need from a relationship?

S: If you do lean towards people-pleasing, you might even have developed a certain style based on what your boyfriend or friends like to see you in, and that can go a long way in guiding how you dress. 'My boyfriend doesn't like short nails, so I wear acrylics.' That is not the same as liking acrylics.

C: 'He says he prefers me when I'm a brunette, so I'm a brunette.' Or, 'I wear my hair long because he says he likes long hair.' It can apply to nearly everything in terms of taste and your likes and dislikes.

S: So, when you come out of those relationships, you can be left with all these preferences that have been totally influenced and dominated by someone else, to the extent that you don't know what you actually like any more. How do *you* feel good? What do *you* enjoy?

C: It's easy to go down this route when you're younger, but you should never do what other people want you to do when you want to do something else. If someone tries to pressure you to do things their way instead of yours, just think, *Fuck off!*

S: I do think it's important to acknowledge that you have different friends for different things in life. Perhaps your current friends have different aspirations or lifestyles to you, but are they kind? Good friends go a long way in terms of self-love and support, which is why you should really cherish the solid friendships that you have, even if there are just one or two people. Often when people get into relationships, they're like, I want to make my boyfriend so happy, and I want to make all this effort, and that is all good. But you need to put that same energy into your friendships because they're just as, if not more, important, especially when you're young.

C: Because the thing is, boys do come and go. It's just fact. I mean, we all hope that one of them will stay around at some point, but generally, relationships at this age are short lived. My parents always told me that they both had loads of boyfriends and girlfriends before they met each other, and you do have to remind yourself that, yes, you value your relationship, but your friendships are the support system that will be there for you, no matter what happens.

S: You do have to learn to assert yourself and your own needs in how you build your social circle, though. When we were younger, it was like we always needed to have a plan, we always wanted to be out and be social butterflies. It would be, 'What are we doing tonight?' And if you had no plans, then it was, 'What am I doing with my life? Everyone else is out.' But now we have absolutely accepted that we are happiest with a small circle of friends and quality over quantity. Having three or four close friends can be so much more valuable to us than twenty or thirty acquaintances.

C: I think we also had to learn how to say no when we didn't want to do something socially. Being able to say, 'No, I don't want to do that on Saturday night,' or 'No, I don't fancy that for lunch on Tuesday,' is something really vital. In the past, we may have said yes to things out of a sense of FOMO (fear of missing out). But it is absolutely OK and acceptable to decline an invitation to anything and you are under no obligation to continually meet new people. This idea that you must be a loser if you don't know 800 people is just madness. By stating your needs, setting your boundaries and communicating what you want, you are conserving your energy for everything that you hope to achieve, instead of spending it all on pleasing other people.

S: If it costs you your peace, it's too expensive.

C: You are also learning how to put yourself first, which as young women is something that can be culturally really hard to do, because it's just expected that we will go along with whatever is best for other people. The problem is, that while you're busy serving other people's needs, yours will be neglected.

If being by yourself at home, watching *Friends* all night, is what you want to do, no one should make you feel bad about that. And if they do try to make you feel bad about it, you should definitely have a chat with them about it, because it's not on. No one should make you feel like shit for doing what you want to do. Ever.

S: Keep a good eye on the kind of friends who try to guilt you into doing things or make you feel bad for not wanting to do X, Y or Z, because that is definitely a red flag. In fact, one of the most important gifts you can give to yourself as you become more self-aware and know more about who you are and what you need, is to look at the relationships in your life and be honest about them. If like you say you are drifting from your group, is it all of your friends or just some of them?

C: Are these relationships serving you? It's an entirely legitimate question to ask. While you are being honest with yourself about your goals and needs, it is definitely acceptable to consider if your life would be better without some of the relationships you currently have. I wish we had understood that it wasn't the end of the world when some relationships break down. From sixteen to twenty-five, you go through a huge transition, and there is so much in flux in every single part of your life.

S: So, it's totally normal for relationships to be ending and new ones starting during that period. Or for some friendships to be falling apart, to make space for new ones. Judge your happiness in *any* kind of relationship right in *this* moment. But in saying that, don't ever feel you have to cut off *everyone* who has been in your life all these years in order to move forward, because you risk losing people who are actually your roots as well. It's not a question of one or the other.

C: When considering this kind of break, it's always best to take where you are now as the evidence. Forget all the history. Is this a healthy, balanced, functional relationship? Yes, of course, you have to consider any mitigating factors that might be influencing someone's behaviour. But also, be honest – have these factors led you to excuse poor treatment for a really long time? Can you imagine anything changing, or are you both stuck in a negative cycle?

S: While it's hard to do, you have to forget the good times in the long-distant past and face up to the current reality.

If it costs you your peace, it's too expensive.

C: If you met your friend or boyfriend now, would you still choose to let them into your life? Would you pursue them? If the answer is no, you can't let history dictate your present. Obviously, ending any kind of relationship when you realise it is no longer right for you is painful. Friendship break-ups are probably the hardest.

S: There's a certain level of expectation that romantic relationships are going to end at some point. We have all watched enough romantic break-ups in films and listened to break-up songs, but you hear way less about the breakdown of friendships.

C: If you do decide to break up with any of your friends, there is the chance that you're going to come out of it looking unkind or mean, because we don't have quite the same attitude to a woman choosing to exclude another woman from her life, even if it is for her own emotional health. It's easy for others to say that you're a bitch because you've 'dropped' a friend, but the reality is that she might have been draining you dry for years, and no one else really had any idea what was going on.

S: With friendship break-ups, it all depends on the circumstances. If you're in a group of six and there is one toxic girl in there that you don't want to be friends with any more, you need to be very mindful of the way you deal with the situation. You need to stay civil and respectful, and we would recommend taking a light touch, rather than announcing that you don't want to be her friend any more. Instead, aim to create distance and boundaries. Steer towards the other members of the group, while keeping the toxic person at arm's length. It may sometimes feel disingenuous, but treading softly-softly may end in a better result for you – because there are other people involved, and group dynamics can be pretty fragile.

C: If it's a solo friend, I do truly believe that honesty is the best policy. Say it was me and you, Soph. I mean, I think you would need to have a proper conversation to convey why you didn't want to continue this relationship.

S: Imagine.

C: I know. But you know otherwise there is going to be way more confusion, and things can get very messy. I think you have to treat it like a romantic break-up, with full respect and clarity.

S: With close friends you have shared so much love with, and you do care about, it can be incredibly hard to draw those lines if you feel the relationship no longer brings anything positive to your life. That doesn't mean that you can't look back with good memories and feel fond about your experiences together. But if you don't miss them from your life and if they are consistently taking much, much more than they offer in return, it is the right call to move on.

C: I do think that any friend who endlessly makes constant negative demands on your energy without giving anything back is someone you need to consider moving away from.

S: I so agree – my dad always says that people are either radiators or drains. Radiators give you warmth, whereas drains suck the life out of you. As you get to know yourself more and more, remember that you are hugely impacted by the company you keep, so the people around you can have a big influence on how you feel about yourself and the direction you will go in the future. Seek out the radiators – they are the ones worth manifesting.

Dilemma Three

When I look around, all my friends are in great jobs or on the path to a great job that they love, they all have boyfriends and one is even engaged now. I just feel like I'm so behind at this point, I'm never going to be able to catch up – what can I do to get my life back on track?

S: God, comparison can really be the thief of joy, can't it? Who hasn't felt like you? It's like we live in an era where everyone is always looking in from the outside on everyone else's journey and making so many judgements about where they should be depending on other people around them, which is so silly when you really think about it.

C: I do think it's hard for all of us to enjoy life as it's happening these days. This sense of waiting for the next high and the next thing on the tick list, can make it so hard to appreciate being in the present! Social media contributes to that, and we struggle with that too. You might be having a really good day, or be out for dinner, and having a lovely time. But then you flick through your phone and suddenly you feel like what you're doing isn't enough and negativity can take over.

It can so easily seem like others are ahead of you in life, which in turn makes you feel like you are behind. And that is just *so* not true. You have to try to stop those thoughts from developing any further and steer them along more rational lines, because you are still on *your own* journey, which is a totally different path, completely unrelated to anyone else's, and you will find your way; it just might take a little more time.

S: On our podcast and YouTube, we always say that you can only work to the pace of your own clock. We do get a lot of people writing into the podcast who tell us that they are struggling with similar feelings and that they feel lost with where they are going and who they are. They might feel that they don't know what they're doing with their lives because they're single, or they don't enjoy their jobs or are generally unfulfilled. In those instances, it's very easy to feel that you're behind in life.

C: There is just so much pressure.

S: But there's just no such thing as being behind in life. It doesn't exist!

C: I think it starts when you leave school, and it seems like you're all on the same level playing field. Then it can feel like this kind of race begins, who can get ahead the quickest? Who is going to get the first job? Who is going to get the first engagement ring or house or baby?

S: There are videos of us online saying that we wanted to be pregnant by the time we were twenty-five and be living with our partners, and now it's like, *Jesus Christ, who made those expectations?* There's another video deep in the archive where I say that if I'm not with my fiancé at twenty-five, I'm going to be so stressed that my life is falling apart. It's like, *What were we thinking?*

C: That just shows how things change and how all these age milestones that you have in your head when you are young are completely random and not based on anything.

S: We always say that we have heroes who made it in their forties, and you can create a million-pound business in your fifties. There is such a long runway to achieve all sorts of things in our life, so we definitely all collectively need to take a breath with it.

C: The relationship race is the same. First kiss, who is going to lose their virginity first, who is going to get a boyfriend first, who is going to move in together. There's this weird clock-watching, which is just so ridiculous because (as we have found out) you just can't plan when you are going to meet someone, how long it will last, or the speed at which the relationship will progress. You are just not in control of these things, though you can, of course, manifest them into your life over time.

If you are single and you have to socialise with lots of couples and they're asking you who's on the cards and you're thinking, *There is literally no one on the cards. Just let me be*, it can be really challenging. Likewise, when your friends are all seemingly doing well in their jobs and you are struggling to make headway; we absolutely would never want to minimise that. Comparison can become so loud, especially when you so want something that feels out of reach.

S: We've both definitely had setbacks and heartache, and sad times too. But we do actively try to keep focused on the positives. Instead of *Why haven't I got X or Y?*, we always turn it around into *Aren't I lucky to have Z?!* Gratitude and manifesting aren't going to stop the difficult moments, but I do think it helps you get back onto your own personal tracks and allows you to accept that life will come at you when it's meant to.

There's no such thing as being behind in life. It doesn't exist!

Dilemma Four

I have always felt this need to be popular as long as I can remember. At high school it was something that I obsessed about and now as an adult, I'm really struggling with people-pleasing and I find it so difficult to say no to basically anything social. I find that I'm constantly exhausted from going out all the time, so much so that I can't focus at work and I rarely *really* enjoy myself. How do I say no without letting my friends down?

C: I think the problem here is the question. Saying no to going out if you're knackered is letting precisely no one down. It is simply self-care. So, the fact that you feel like you're letting people down – or you're being made to feel like you're letting people down – just because you take care of yourself, is something you need to really look at. As we mature, life responsibilities start to come into play and that can mean redefining the dynamics of all sorts of relationships. Putting yourself first has to be your priority. There is no way you are going to achieve all of your personal goals if all you're doing is chasing validation from other people.

This is the stage of life when it becomes harder to keep up lots and lots of relationships with every single friend you have ever had, and that is why it's natural to start to boil it down to the people you feel most connected and close to. Aside from Soph, I've also got two sisters and a couple more friends whom I care deeply about. Then I've also got to dedicate time to my boyfriend. I often feel like I can barely keep up with the people I have in my life already! Honest to God! The stress. So, I'm not frantically trying to make friends. For me personally, I'm going to try to safeguard and cherish the circle I have rather than trying to appear popular or be out every night of the week with a different girl. Of course, things will change over time and more good people will come into our lives and that is wonderful. Perhaps in the next five years there will be a few more people to keep up with, and that's plenty.

S: The other thing about friends – and this is something we have spoken about on the podcast – is that they won't always be as important to your day-to-day life as they are now. One of our guests explained that when you're younger, your whole twenties is about mates. It's all about going out with friends, to the pub, to a party, and spending all this time together. But then when she hit her thirties, she found that her life became more about her home and her partner. She still sees her friends on occasion, but they are not as involved in her life as they once were.

C: While you can believe that your friends are everything, life does get involved. People move, have kids, change jobs . . . They won't always be around like they are now. Being popular just won't matter in the same way. But, what *is* everything, is your relationship with yourself, because you aren't going anywhere. Investing time and energy into your own well-being and goals is the most important thing you can do right now. Of course, your true friends will always be around. You might not speak to them every day in the same way that you do now, but they will always be there in your life.

S: One of our friends now lives in LA and we haven't seen her in over six months. But when we FaceTime her, it is as if we have never been apart. True friendships don't need constant maintenance, but as long as you cherish them and make each other feel valued and cared for, they will continue to play a part in your life. Self-love, self-care, self-esteem, self-worth, knowing yourself; all of it is a massive process, and there's also no rush to get everything figured out.

C: We can sit here and offer the advice that we have here, but in five years we could look back and think some of the things we have said were a mistake. Because, obviously, we are going to keep on growing and developing, and our relationships with ourselves will continue to shift. If we look back to a couple of years ago, we didn't realise that we had no idea what we were doing and we were approaching lots of situations from the wrong direction. But that was because we hadn't developed our self-worth and understanding to where it is now. You can only work with what you have.

S: Change is inevitable, and it's something you should welcome into your life. A lot of things we manifest will make significant changes to our lives and shift the dynamics of all sorts of relationships. But as long as we both stay true to ourselves, we hope we will always be able to navigate whatever comes our way.

How to make a manifestation board

We do a board every year. You can refresh it: use a pinboard, take off the goals you have achieved, and add more.

Materials you need

Paper
Glue
Scissors
A stack of magazines

Method

Call your bestie, clear your afternoon and get crafty by making a manifestation board.

Cut out a selection of images that represent your goals and the things you would love to achieve. You can put anything on your board. It could be a house, a family, an engagement ring – and they don't have to be things that you want instantly. It's your board, so you can put on anything you are attracted to.

If there is anything specific that you really want to achieve – say starting a new business – put the logo on the board.

The pictures can resemble something completely different in your mind than in someone else's – it's something entirely personal.

Stick your board on your fridge or above your bed – anywhere you will be seeing it every day. If you're looking at your goals daily it helps keep them alive.

What's on our manifestation board

A London flat

A quote about keeping motivated

Two girls jumping into the sea

A girl with loads of suitcases

A successful woman at her laptop in an office

A range of inspirational women we personally
  look up to

Favourite self-care rituals

Cinzia

- For me it's all about a daily bath.

- If it's a real pamper sesh, I'll add salts to the bath, get a Garnier sheet mask on. And then after, it'll be dressing gown on, pressing play on my favourite show or YouTuber.

- Self-care can be just turning your phone off for a while. Winding down and disconnecting from whatever has stressed you that day is so important, so make sure you switch your phone off at least an hour before you get into your bed.

Sophia

■ I love to take an early-evening walk to clear my head after a day on my computer or running around, and dust off the cobwebs.

■ For me, nothing beats feeling clean and relaxing in a clean space. I like to brew a tea and get out an array of snacks and get in my bed in my dressing gown and watch *Friends*.

■ Unfollowing people who are bringing you down, or not providing you with content that uplifts you or serves a purpose for you, is a step towards self-care.

How to decorate your space

WE LOVE THE SCANDINAVIAN STYLE OF HOME DECOR. In terms of palette, we always go for neutrals, and we love wood for making a space feel homey. We also love natural linen to add some texture to both our bedding and soft furnishings.

CONSIDER ADDING GREENERY AND PLANTS TO YOUR SPACE. Indoor plants have been proven to improve concentration and productivity by up to 15 per cent.

NATURAL LIGHT IS SO IMPORTANT. A bright space, even if it's tiny, will make you feel more at peace.

CLEAN YOUR SPACE, CLEAR YOUR MIND. We like to keep our space clutter-free and are religious about clearing out and recycling things. Don't let things pile up, and donate things that you aren't using.

ADD ELEMENTS THAT INSPIRE YOU. Look to add artwork that makes you happy and can help you manifest, and make progress towards your goals.

Fun Friday night: your cosmic future

So, you're home alone. It's Friday night and according to Instagram the rest of the *world* is having a better time than you. Well, fear not, my friend, because we have an activity that will not only make the hours of Friday night fly by, but will also hopefully give you a little insight into yourself.

Now, I know what you're thinking. *Astrology is a sham, isn't it?* Well, we can see where you're coming from, especially if you're talking about the kind of advice you find in the back of a magazine. But we like to take the positives from everything we encounter, and Sophia in particular has become interested in cosmic alignment.

'Cosmic what?' we hear you ask. Well, we have learnt that it's better to think of astrology as an ancient practice that extends way beyond your personal horoscope. Astrology is much more about the relationships (see what we've done there) between the planets and the way they move, rather than, say, thinking that all Sagittarius boys are commitmentphobes.

Your astrological birth chart is a snapshot of the sky at the exact time and location that you were born. It's like a little map of the sun, the moon and the planets. There are plenty of websites (try cafeastrology.com or astro.com) that allow you to input the

information of where and when you were born, to get your birth chart. From there you have the basis of your primal triad – your sun, your moon and your ascendant or 'rising' sign. Your sun sign you will probably already know – it's the one that depends on the day you were born and most represents your overall personality. Your moon sign is the zodiac sign in which the moon was positioned in the moment you were born and is more related to your emotional self and mood, and often provides a really good clue to what will make you feel most fulfilled. Your rising sign is how other people perceive you – basically your social mask – and will most often be quite different from your actual personality.

Whether you choose to research more online or in a book, diving deeper into the corners of your personality can help you make more sense of your own behaviour and help you find some self-acceptance. None of us have only 'positive' elements to our birth charts, and confronting some of your failings (even if everything your birth chart says doesn't tally with you) can be cathartic. No one is perfect, and astrology shows us – if nothing else – how uniquely imperfect we all are. Whether you believe that your future is in the stars or not, even identifying what you do and don't agree with is an exercise in itself.

Connecting with your inner voice

1

Everyone struggles with connecting to their intuition. But trusting your instincts and understanding your thoughts is so important – and generally the most valid and the clearest reflection of what you believe in. Yes, you can rationalise, but that immediate reaction you have can be an important guide to the right choice.

2

Doubting your gut instinct is where so many things go wrong. Try not to constantly second-guess yourself.

3

The hardest thing is to stop yourself being swayed by other people's influence and opinions. Don't trick yourself into thinking that the people's opinions around you are your opinions. That's easily done.

4 You may very well find you have a new surge of individuality after a relationship ends, but seismic shifts can also leave you feeling at sea and struggling to connect with your intuition. Give yourself time to re-tune into your internal weathervane and embrace the opportunity to experiment and find out what you really want. When you were in a relationship, perhaps you always went to eat at your boyfriend's favourite restaurant, but now go and try ten different places to see what floats *your* boat.

5 Give yourself the space to sit with your feelings and mull them over, but always set a time limit. Say to yourself, 'In three months' time I will have made this decision.' If you're still feeling the same way, with the same doubts, then act on it. Hold yourself accountable to the time crunch. Because otherwise, you will find yourself still stewing for months or even years.

6 It can take time to find the answer to any question. Don't make snap choices, and try never to make permanent decisions from temporary emotions. Let your feelings rise and ensure it's not just a phase or a fleeting feeling.

The best way to exercise

What we've learnt when it comes to exercise is that you really need to find something you like, because then it stops feeling like a chore. We started going to the gym together when we were sixteen. Because of ballet, we were always active, but when we stopped classes, we wanted to fill the gap after school. Right from the beginning, we've always been very consistent, but we have changed what we do a lot over the years.

IT DOESN'T ALWAYS HAVE TO BE CARDIO. When we started, everything we did was very cardio-based. We'd do half an hour on the bikes, half an hour of running and then a HIIT circuit. It was just too much, looking back, and we weren't always enjoying it. By the time we were eighteen, we had started doing weights, following fitness influencers and their plans, to educate ourselves. Now we are confident, and we can create our own workouts, so that is a really great way to get started.

KEEP THINGS INTERESTING. Switching up your routine is also a good idea. We would go to the gym five times a week and do: legs, arms, back; legs, arms, back. But once you've done that for a couple of months, you're like, *Fuck, not this again*. It's so repetitive. And then, of course, you find yourself losing motivation The best thing to do is to switch up your routine regularly. Adding in skipping, rowing, or different weight machines that you haven't tried before, can revitalise your workout and make you feel driven to be there.

WORKING OUT WILL GIVE YOU ENDORPHINS AND CHANGE YOUR MOOD. On the days when we don't work out, we have realised we just don't feel as good. We aren't as focused or content, because exercise gives you energy, but also calms your mind at the same time. It can even be as small as going for a walk. It plays such a vital part in your mental health by boosting your mood throughout the day. No matter what else happens, at least you know you've had a good workout.

THINK ABOUT HOW YOU FEEL, NOT JUST HOW YOU LOOK. People need to not put so much pressure on looking super fit. We don't go to the gym to be shredded or thin, we go to feel good. The endorphins are addictive. Even if you just go and walk on the treadmill for twenty minutes, that can make you feel ten times better. You *don't* have to go and come away in pain or exhausted, you can just go and move your body and you will feel the benefits of that all day. It's nice to feel healthy and strong, knowing that you're treating your body with kindness. We find that reflects on so many levels.

BE PATIENT WITH YOURSELF. It can be really hard to get back on the exercise wagon after you've fallen off. After a longer break, you wonder how you could possibly have ever gone five times a week. When you're on the wagon, it's just part of your routine and you don't even think about it. But when you get out of the habit, it can seem unmanageable. Don't beat yourself up too much if you're struggling to get into a routine or maintain discipline. Be kind to yourself, and let yourself have down days without guilt. Regular exercise is something you have to build up to, and we all need days when we do nothing, switch off and recharge.

The Most Important Relationship of All

CHAPTER SIX

The Shape of Healthy Relationships

So, after all of this discussion, we wanted to leave you with a really clear idea of what a healthy relationship should look like, because we both think that there is just such an absence of information on the topic out there. When it comes to romance, it's like every romcom or romantic novel seems to cover what meeting someone will be like, and you get a fairly distinct run-through of the early-day dramas. But what about the bit that comes after? The more mundane day-in, day-out shape of an actual relationship? The part beyond the 'honeymoon phase'? It's something that's brought up so rarely.

We both felt totally lost when we first got into relationships – we didn't really understand how we should be treated, what we should feel, or what would be important to make them last. Then when things went wrong, we thought *we* were to blame, that if only we'd tried harder, or compromised more, we could have made it work. But actually, it was very clear – to anyone even slightly removed from the situation – that some of these relationships were doomed from the start. As always, it is far easier to preach than to practise, and as soon as you have your emotions entwined in something, everything can get very foggy, even when you have answered as many dilemmas as we have. We all learn lessons along the way, and rather than dwelling on our past experiences as mistakes or a waste of our time, we take them as signposts pointing us firmly towards our goals.

Now that we are both in what we would describe as healthy, romantic, platonic and professional relationships, we can definitely see some things more clearly. We're all different, but there are some basic foundations that both sides of a relationship need – and deserve – to build on together.

Dilemma One

I see my boyfriend throughout the week, but I feel like we rarely connect. We are either shattered getting up early for work or else back home, tired in the evenings, and there never seems to be that sense of being special to each other. I can't complain that we aren't physically spending the hours together, because we are, I just feel like he saves the best of himself for other people and I get the dregs. He never asks me about my life or job or seems in any way engaged with things that are important to me and it is slowly sapping my confidence in myself.

C: Firstly, as a progression from investing time in yourself and finding clarity in your goals and needs, it's so important, right from the beginning of any relationship, that you are aware of what it is that makes *you* happy. For me personally, spending quality time with my partner is the absolute most important aspect – that is what makes me feel valued and special and it sounds like you are similar. When I say quality time, I don't mean crazy plans or anything like that. It can just be agreeing to watch a film together and putting our phones away. Or just sitting at home and having a meal together at the table instead of in front of the TV. It's the feeling of being connected with your partner that means so much. The time together that you describe spending with your boyfriend is just not quality time. You need some good dates, some lovely weekend time, and you should never feel like you're being shoehorned into someone else's schedule. When you're talking about the shape of a healthy relationship, connected, quality time is an absolute must.

S: But it's also true that everyone is different in terms of what they prioritise in their relationship and how they give and receive love. While I obviously need quality time too, for me, what is most important is feeling supported by my partner in terms of how he helps me on a day-to-day basis. That is what makes me feel the most cherished. In order to do that, a partner needs to be engaged with your life and passions. They have to listen enough to understand what is going on with you, so they are able to support your endeavours and contribute, if they can. For me, it is all about the feeling that you are constantly being offered support without them ever making a big deal about it. It could be tiny things, like sending ideas for the podcast or helping me find something I need for an event.

A partner needs to be engaged with your life and passions.

C: It could be as small as offering to cook dinner if I'm working late and waiting for me to eat it. These aren't huge things, but they mean so much on a daily basis, because they make you feel nurtured.

S: It's absolutely not all about the big gestures (though they're obviously welcome too!), but what we're talking about are the small, everyday reminders that your partner is in your corner and that you're on the same team. They are looking out for you and your interests, every single day. When you haven't had that before, it feels so incredibly different.

C: Now that we both have people in our lives who ask what is going on and want to share advice and are just so supportive, it's hard to imagine not having that. They never undermine or belittle us or our achievements, they just want to help us grow. I get encouragement every single day.

S: And that makes a world of difference. I would also say that another one of the biggest ways that my boyfriend helps me is through the things I've been able to learn from him. Cinzia and I are building this future and a career, but we still don't really know exactly what it's going to look like yet. To have people in our life who can offer guidance by sharing their own experiences is such a huge thing. It makes you feel like you are both paddling your boat in the same direction. And that you have another player flanking you.

C: I think it is worth mentioning that you should never for one second doubt that your partner wants you to succeed. Of course, all this is well and good, but if I'm honest with myself, one of the reasons that my relationship is so much healthier now is because *I'm* addressing doubts like this in a healthier way. Before, in previous relationships, when I felt disrespected or overlooked, I would just swallow it and allow it to change the way I felt about myself – or else mentally, silently note it down. But you can't let it build up to a place where you're ready to explode or it begins to eat away at your self-esteem as you describe. You need to address the small things and your feelings, however insignificant they might seem, head on, there and then.

S: It's so basic, but communication is so important in relationships, especially when you are figuring things out. That is something I do really struggle with and I'm only now gaining the confidence to speak out when something might have hurt me.

C: Knowing that you have a safe space between you where you can express your feelings can definitely give you more confidence to share them. More than the lack of quality time, I think the thing that you need to think about the most is how you can open the channels of communication between the two of you. Perhaps he is feeling something similar, or perhaps he just doesn't have the capacity to fulfil your needs in this way. Maybe you are scared of bringing it up in case it rocks the boat and even though you're not happy, it can sometimes feel like better the devil you know. What is for sure is that this situation won't improve on its own. Communicating your needs to your partner isn't being demanding, it is a vital part of any functioning relationship.

Dilemma Two

After uni my boyfriend and I moved to London together and while I love him, since we've been here, I've realised we have very different ambitions in life. I want to build a career and a home here, see the world and would potentially settle for good. In contrast, he really isn't enjoying living down south and talks about moving home and being closer to his family all the time. I feel like I want more experiences in my life before I even consider moving back to my home town, but he thinks I'm being impractical and not thinking about the financial realities.

S: Having similar ambitions is such an important factor when it comes to relationships. When you're seventeen, you're not thinking intently about your life aspirations, because you're not sure what they are yet, so the idea of complementing life goals is just not on your radar. You're just thinking, *Is he fit?* But pretty quickly, your priorities in what you are looking for in a partner begin to change as you learn more about yourself and what you value.

C: Having someone who is adventurous and driven to take all sorts of crazy opportunities is something that is really important to us. As we are so goal orientated, it is also really important that we have partners who are similar in that sense, and we love the idea that we are building a brand new life together – that's what motivates us to get up and going in the morning. What we have realised is that we need to be with someone who is excited to be part of that ride and have dreams that dovetail with that attitude to life.

S: That's not necessarily for everyone. There will be people out there looking for a partner who is ultra-passionate about building a life close to family and everything they have grown up with like your boyfriend. There's a lot of stability and security in knowing that there aren't going to be these big, overwhelming changes, like moving cities and starting life all over again, away from your people, your tribe. Neither of these two versions of how you could choose to live your life are better or worse than the other. It's absolutely not *this person is ambitious to build an empire and live in LA, so they are better than someone who wants to live on the same street as their parents and work for the family business.* It really is horses for courses, and there are going to be plenty of girls or guys out there who share the traits you value in yourself and have similar life aspirations – the key is finding a partner who encourages and brings even more energy to your dreams, instead of making you feel like you're being held back.

While it can be hard to talk about, financial realities are also really important in any relationship. If you are a big saver and you are with someone who is more YOLO (you only live once), or someone who regularly overspends and ends up in debt, that is going to put a huge pressure on the relationship. There are also still many men who are hard wired to be threatened by a financially successful young woman. That is just a depressing fact of life.

C: We do not need a man to provide for us in a material sense.

S: Hell, yeah! But that can be emasculating for some men.

C: One thousand per cent. Early on in your career when you are just finding your way, a more traditional boyfriend might be comfortable with a parity of income, or with you bringing home less than him. But if your manifestations pay off, and it tips into a place where you are financially self-sufficient, that can really upturn the power balance.

S: Even if there is a disparity in earnings between you and your partner, financial conversations should be open, respectful and supportive. If one of you can't afford something, but the other is able to cover it, then you need to consider agreeing on a way that works for both of you. Ultimately, you need to see yourselves as a team. But equally, the partner who is earning less should always do their best to be generous in whichever way they are able to, and not start expecting to have a free ride at every juncture. If you're still young and not married, when it comes to conversations about mortgages or more important things in your future, there should be an understanding that each of you is responsible for protecting their assets. It's not personal, it's just being sensible.

In an ideal world, absolutely everything between you and your partner would be split 50/50, but if not, you have to try to be as transparent as possible, to ensure that no one feels taken advantage of. And if a guy is intimidated by either your financial or career success? If they don't want to hear the details of your work or cheer you on when you're doing well? That is all on him. You have to remember that your success has the potential to bring out uncertainties in someone who isn't secure. He absolutely shouldn't be taking that out on you, but it would be naïve to think that female financial freedom doesn't threaten some men.

It sounds very much like you both have competing rather than complementary aspirations. I think it's really telling that he describes your dreams of building your life away from your home town as unrealistic, because you still have so far to go in both of your careers, who knows what the next few years might bring? But there are also always compromises to be made for love and no one can ever make that decision for you.

Dilemma Three

My best friends and I have known each other since primary school and I love them all so dearly. But these days, with work and boyfriends, it seems like we can't find time for each other and we can go weeks without even speaking more than a few group WhatsApps. I know you guys work together, but have you ever felt your relationship drift and how have you pulled it back?

C: I honestly think there's a big misunderstanding about what true friendship can look like in the long-term context.

S: I agree. Long-term friendship is not all group holidays and having kids who go to school with each other. We always say that friendships are like stories – they have chapters and phases and are *always* evolving.

C: They're also not always lovey-dovey and intense. I mean, I don't like Sophia to touch me.

S: *Eugh!* We don't, like, text each other. There's no 'How's your day?' or checking in or catching up every day like you might with someone you had met more recently.

C: It's more, 'I'll see you when I see you.'

S: When Cinz goes on holiday, I'm always like, 'See ya, have a good time!' I am not texting her to find out what she's been doing. Healthy friendships on a long-term basis need space and are not codependent. The minute they go away, you can't be trying to FaceTime them. It all goes back to being happy in your own company.

C: I think long-term friendships are more about reaching a stage where you can read each other very well and you can lean in and lean out of the absolute trust that you have between yourselves. When Sophia is pissed off, I will know. She doesn't have to say anything.

S: Likewise.

C: If she's in a bad mood or upset, I can almost read her body language. I'm like, 'She's going to cry in 3 . . . 2 . . . 1 . . . waterworks.'

S: Well, I can do that when I know you're going to be sick. We were coming in from a night out – it was actually the first night that our boyfriends met, and we were in a taxi on the way home. And I just looked at Cinzia and I said, 'She's going to throw up.' And the boys were like, 'Noooo, she's totally fine, don't worry.' And I literally went, 'She's going to throw up in 3 . . . 2 . . . 1 . . .' And she did. It was like a film; I couldn't believe it myself. With us, because we have been friends for so long, it's like a sisterly, sibling relationship for sure.

Deep down, our friendship is based on the knowledge that we know we always, always have each other's best interests at heart. We have this years-long friendship, we know we're *in* it. It's not like we need to discuss anything. I do think that one of the reasons we've always gravitated towards each other is that we aren't demanding of each other's time. Also, neither of us thrives in dramatic or bitchy environments. We've never had that dynamic. Like, we would never have an issue over a boy or anything like that.

C: Absolutely not.

S: We get that a lot on the podcast: people asking us if we've ever liked the same boy. And all these stories about 'me and my best friend sleeping with the same boy'. We would just never.

C: Firstly, we have completely different tastes, and secondly, even when we were younger and didn't know what our tastes really were, we still knew it was an unwritten rule that you must follow. When we're talking about crossing lines, my God, this is a line. It's weird if you're trying to pursue a guy that you know your friend fancies. That's just a rogue move.

S: I think that's another key to our friendship: we have never seen each other as competition. We're both just girls' girls, and we always have been, which is why we have an easy ride. We just don't have to try too hard. I mean, we can sit in silence for hours, and it's not a thing.

C: Oh yeah, we rarely talk to each other.

S: I wouldn't even notice that it was silence. But of *course*, we have had phases in our friendship – and while I like to think we will always be besties, life does sometimes change things. When you are at school, you all have the same lives, you all know the same people. Everyone is on the same schedule. But then, as you grow up and you transition into adulthood, new people walk into your

Friendships ebb and flow but it's important to make an effort when you can.

life, who perhaps come from different places and backgrounds. They come with different influences, and your old friends won't know or perhaps understand how these people have changed your life. When you add in moving to different spaces and places, to unis and offices, it's obvious why things shift or drift a bit as you describe. Feeling out of sync is totally natural, because you need to pursue your own life.

C: While it can feel sad, I think it's so important to say, don't stress about it. I think about my mum and her best friend, they sometimes go years without seeing each other. They might have a phone call here and there, but when they do see each other they just click back into place. They haven't fallen out, and they don't love each other any less when time passes between them. They just have busy lives. Adult friendships can't function in that inside-each-other's-pocket way.

S: We often get dilemmas that are centred around this moment in life. Often, it's one friend feeling like another has left her behind. She will say, 'I'm making all of this effort and arranging things with my friend and she's constantly cancelling. And it looks like she doesn't care about me any more.' People often ask if they should continue to try to keep their friendship going or just leave it. We always say that it may just be a signal that your friendship is entering a new phase. You cannot always align with someone else, because it's not like a boyfriend–girlfriend relationship, and sometimes one or the other of you needs the space to explore and experiment with a new version of themselves. But it doesn't mean you can't be friends any more.

C: Friendships ebb and flow. Take our friends Summer and Naomi as an example. Before, we would see Naomi quite a bit, we'd always be going up to Manchester to meet her. But now she's moved to LA, we're on different time zones, so of course, we're not really speaking as often. We will visit her at some point, and it will be back to how it always was, but that contact has changed. Whereas her sister Summer, we only used to see her once every three or four months. But now we've moved into the same building as her, that will obviously mean we will be closer friendship-wise. But again, that won't last for ever, because who knows how long we will all be living here.

S: Cinzia and I are very fortunate that our lives have stayed in sync, because we are still on very similar schedules. We have the same job, we know a lot of the same people, and our lives are very entwined. If Cinzia had gone on to work at a safari park and I'd gone to work at a university, and we were living at opposite ends of the country, our relationship would be different. Not worse or better but different. We would probably have big, long catch-ups and have reunions every few months. We probably wouldn't sit in a room in silence for hours with each other because there would be more to say.

C: But it should go without saying that in any relationship, including old friendships, there is work to be done on both sides. No one wants to feel that their friend doesn't care about them any more.

S: So, it's about making an effort with people where you can. Sometimes it's like a seesaw, and one person might be making more of an effort than the other, but that can change and swap around over time. As a whole, as long as it's fairly balanced, it shows you have found a healthy way to keep each other in your lives.

C: And making an effort doesn't necessarily mean getting all dressed up and going out to somewhere special and spending money. It can just be going to each other's house and doing the shop together, then getting a takeaway and chatting shit all night.

S: We don't need to spend money to have a nice time with our friends. We can sit in front of Netflix and have the best night ever. I think that because, just like everyone, we don't really document that kind of time as much online, it isn't as visible. I guess it's not seen as exciting or Instagramable. It's not like, 'Look, I'm out doing this, wearing that.' But that kind of time is so important for your friendship.

Dilemma Three

Last year I really let one of my closest friends down. She lost her mum quite suddenly and I dealt with it really badly and didn't show up for her like I should have. I feel a heavy sense of guilt about that still to this day and I'm desperate to rebuild bridges because she is one of the best people in my life. We see each other fairly often, but it's just not the same and I'm just not sure how to fix it.

S: We have definitely made friendship mistakes in the past. There are times when we now see we could have communicated better with each other and been more frank in expressing our feelings. There's nothing you can do about the past, except for changing your attitude and behaviour going forward. I think when you look at mistakes you've made, you have to remember that at that moment in time, that is what you wanted or decided to do, so you can't regret it. You just have to one hundred per cent own your mistake and work on rebuilding the trust you once had. Have you told her how sorry you are about how it all went down? Because this is something that really needs to be communicated in a straightforward way.

C: Soph and I have never had a situation like yours, but we definitely lost track of our friendship because of a lack of communication when we were in previous relationships and I think it is so common to feel you've got to a point where you feel you physically can't say what needs to be said. Now that we're in new relationships, we have prioritised our friendship within that. Right from the outset, it's been made abundantly clear that we're going to hang out as a four, and those boys are going to know each other, because we do not want history to repeat itself.

S: Going forward, any boyfriend I have is going to know Cinzia and her partner, because this girl is the most important thing to me. You can definitely learn and move on from your mistakes, and in fact, it can make your friendship even stronger than it was before, because you have proven it can weather a storm.

Dilemma Four

My best friend has recently started dating an absolute creep. That's not me being jealous or overprotective, by any measure he is a horror. All our friends feel the same way and I am totally lost about how to navigate it. Should I be honest? I'm so scared that it will make her turn away from me.

S: This is a real tough one. Because there must be something that your friend sees in this guy and when you boil it down, she's the only one dating him, so her opinion on his character is the only one that matters. But that doesn't mean we don't understand how difficult it can be to see your friend with a guy who is a twat.

C: Or not even a twat, just not right for her. You can tell one hundred per cent that he is *not* the one, but you're going to have to deal with it until she realises for herself.

S: You don't want to be patronising, but sometimes you really can see from the outside how things are going to play out, and it can be frustrating to have to put effort into being nice and welcoming to someone you don't like and you know won't be around for ever. You might be able to see the writing on the wall before it even starts. But if someone would have said to me at the beginning of my last relationship, 'This is not for you, you two are completely mismatched,' I would have been like, 'Fucking cheek! You don't know my relationship!'

C: And that is true, you don't know your friend's relationship, only she does. All you can do is give advice when advice is asked for. When your emotions aren't involved and you're not at all invested in this person, it's very easy to have perspective. But she is the one who has to live it. Even if your friend does ask you very specifically and pointedly for advice, you have to accept that she might not like what she hears and she's probably not going to take your advice, at least not immediately. Working through that situation and reaching a decision is something she has to come to herself, and that can take a long time.

S: All you can do is offer support from the sidelines, as incredibly hard as that might be. But bide your time, a twat will always prove himself to be a twat in the end.

All you can do is give advice

when advice is asked for.

Dilemma Five

In my last review, one of the 'anonymous' feedback comments from my colleagues said that they found me 'pushy and inflexible'. I have a feeling I know who wrote it, because one of the men in my team seems to have an issue whenever I bring up new ideas or voice any opinion on our projects. I'm pretty sure he bitches about me behind my back as well. I really don't think I'm particularly pushy, but it's really hit my confidence and I don't know what steps to take next.

C: We have definitely been on a massive journey in terms of learning about healthy professional relationships, and we've found out that the tendency to people-please can be just as relevant in the workplace as it is in your other relationships.

S: Professional relationships can be really hard to gauge when you're a young person. At school you don't have to make 'professional relationships', so it can be really confusing to establish who is your friend and how the whole business environment works. I think when we talk about communication and boundary-setting, what we've realised is that it's just as important to create those in our professional lives as it is for our personal lives.

There have been so many learning curves. While content creation may not always have the best reputation, there is no denying that what we do professionally is successful because of our choices – and we don't just earn money for ourselves but for lots of other people, whether they are in our team or working with us on outside projects. We have a responsibility to our broader team to make the right calls day in, day out. Because we are young females, without the gloss of private school or university, we have found that we are constantly underestimated in business. And because what we do is entertainment, light hearted and fun, there has often been the misconception that we don't deserve to be taken seriously. Yes, we have a good time in our content and we want to provide escapism for our audience. But, fingers crossed, we hope that we are establishing the foundations of a decades-long career (whether that's in content or not, we don't know yet).

C: We have had some major wake-up calls along the way in terms of realising what people think of us and how we need to assert ourselves within our business relationships.

S: With time, our confidence has definitely grown.

C: I think the most important thing is that we've stopped worrying about coming across as 'difficult' or 'hard work'. You can't be so terrified of annoying someone else that you crawl into your shell, because you will never get out of it. The professional environment is just the same as the personal one – you can't people-please and serve yourself at the same time. You have to say no when you need to say no. Obviously, I'm not saying constantly keep having arguments with your boss – that is not the path to a promotion! But if you feel like something is wrong, or you are being compromised in a way you are uncomfortable with, you have to speak up. That may mean engaging one of your senior colleagues to ask for advice on how to handle the atmosphere created by this guy, or even speaking to your HR team.

S: When you try to please everyone else, things most often turn out in ways that you aren't happy with. That has happened to us in the past, and we don't ever want to repeat that. Even if it's going to piss some people off, we need to say, 'I'm sorry to throw a spanner in the works, but this is shit, we need to start again.'

C: A couple of years ago, we might have sat there and thought, *This isn't right, this isn't how we want to do things.* But we might not have spoken up.

S: Because these people are older than us and they have credentials.

C: But now, if we don't want to do something, we are not going to do it. If it feels wrong, it's a no.

S: In the context of what we do, the reality is that we're the ones that are going to have to deal with the consequences of poor decisions. If something isn't the way we want it, or doesn't reflect what we believe in, we will not do it, no matter who thinks we're twats.

C: Putting yourself first works in *any* scenario, and the more you say no, the easier it gets. The less uncomfortable you feel with saying, 'My interests are important,' the more likely it is that you'll stand up for yourself. When you're a young woman, it can be really hard to say no, because you know you may get a reputation for being 'tricky' for just not doing exactly what other people want you to do. You've been trained to say 'Yes, yes, yes,' no matter what the cost to your own sense of peace and your self-esteem.

Work relationships are definitely an area where you need to set more boundaries and be very, very clear.

But we also know at first hand that being submissive and always agreeable doesn't earn you professional respect. We had an experience where we were on a call with two older guys we worked with, they were in their forties and fifties. We were talking about a project we were working on, and we corrected some information that they had presented us with. We were definitely in line to do so, and it was our area of expertise. As we were explaining the error, one of them had their screen on sharing mode, and we saw a bitchy WhatsApp message flash up from one of the guys to the other, saying that we didn't know what we were talking about, that what we were saying didn't make sense, and we were definitely wrong.

S: When I saw it pop up, I was like, *Oh!* And he then quickly stopped sharing. Initially, we didn't say anything, mainly out of shock. That is some childish, unprofessional behaviour, and you don't expect it from adult men with families, talking to us on a Zoom call about a project that they were earning money from because of our platforms. I also think there was an element of embarrassment, and it really brought it home to us that some people do not take us seriously at all.

C: If they're chatting shit about this, what else are they talking about? We've seen it this time, but how many times has it happened behind our backs?

S: Afterwards, we had a discussion about whether or not we should address this and take it to their bosses? And like, report the exchange?

C: In the end, we made the decision together not to say anything. But in retrospect, we both think we should have spoken up.

S: From that point on, we realised that we needed to put our foot down a bit more, be more assertive and authoritative, and not allow anyone to believe that we were just silly girls who didn't know what they were talking about. That 'Oh, we don't want to piss them off so we won't say anything' era was over.

C: They *clearly* did not take us seriously in that moment, even though there was absolutely no reason for anyone to undermine us or suggest that we didn't know what we were talking about. We knew exactly what we were talking about. Goodness me, the cheek! Looking back, I'm shocked again.

S: Obviously, the whole affair is a typical example of what many older men (and sometimes women) think of young women, but gosh, you do become paranoid that maybe they always chat like this. And maybe *everyone* is thinking and saying the same things.

C: That definitely changed how we presented ourselves in meetings. We now walk in with confidence. When we are talking about a project, we clearly lay out our vision and how we want things to look and exactly how we want the process to run. It needs to happen by this date in this way, otherwise it's not going to work for us and we can't work together. And that is just the way it's going to happen.

S: Work relationships are definitely an area where you need to set more boundaries and be very, very clear. You can't tiptoe around, there shouldn't be any unspoken rules. And like every other relationship in your life, if work connections are taking more than they add to your life, you should absolutely feel emboldened to end them and seek employment elsewhere.

C: There is only really one cardinal rule that goes across all the different types of relationships out there. If someone is treating you poorly, they are treating you poorly, whether that's in the office, at a family party, or in your home. Even if it's a blood relation, you have to see the relationship for what it is. Regardless of how long you've known each other or how long you've been together. Or the fact that they're your cousin. Or the fact that it's your dream job.

S: Of course, everyone does compromise, that is just life. And from time to time, disagreements can crop up. But on the whole, your relationships should just make your life better, and they should never feel like a heavy burden to carry. Sometimes with relationships, you make the wrong call. Sometimes you think someone is really great, and two years down the line they prove you wrong. That's fine. It's not about thinking that if you befriend someone or go and work somewhere and it's a mistake, that means you are stupid or you've failed. Sometimes you just give someone a chance who didn't deserve it, and other times it was because that person was only meant to be in your life for a season. We are constantly learning to accept that with grace.

C: We do believe that healthy relationships have to start from a place of power. That means you have to go into things with your eyes open, with a good knowledge of your own self, and the confidence to broach difficult topics, to say no and to clearly communicate your needs. With a new boyfriend, when things are fresh and exciting, it can feel silly to bring up the little grumbles. But raising any issues, no matter how small, is the only way to let your new partner know where they stand: 'I didn't like it when you did that', 'I would feel much more supported if you could be there for me in this way.' People aren't mind readers, so vocalise your boundaries and expectations. You might feel totally, eeek, this is so awkward, but neither Soph nor I are tolerating any poor behaviour ever again, so let's be clear about it right from the start.

Relationships are *everything*. Get them wrong and they can drain your energy, crush your spirit and impact your opportunities, joys and achievements. Get them right and they can level up your life. From how you relate to yourself, to your besties, to your boss or bae, do yourself the service of taking relationships seriously. You deserve only the very best.

Identify how you receive love

It's so important to know what it is that makes you feel loved. When you get into a new relationship, you have to remember that your new partner isn't a mind reader. Unless you tell him what it is you need to feel happy, he's going to be reaching around in the dark. The biggest problem is that most of us have never considered it before.

Here are some ways to help you work out what means the most to you:

- Think about what the nicest thing any partner, friend or family member has ever done for you. What was it that made you feel full and fuzzy? Perhaps they gave you an amazing gift, or an amazing compliment, changed the bedsheets specially for you, or just scheduled quality time?

- If you had to boast about your partner, what would you say? What is it about him that you most value?

- The bottom line is that there are lots of ways to express and receive love, and all of them are great. Whether your partner spends quality time with you, helps you to do things, pays you compliments, makes you feel special with gifts, or creates physical intimacy, it's all amazing. But there will be one way of communicating love that resonates most significantly for you, and if you don't get it, or enough of it, it can lead to you feeling undervalued.

- Often the ways we receive love can come from the way we were raised and loved in our families. Every single morning, Sophia's dad brings her mum a cup of tea, and he's always in the garden, fixing things and using his time to take care of things in the house. Whereas Cinzia grew up in an Italian household where quality time with family was everything. Weekends were spent having family get-togethers and meals, and the whole family was in each other's company all day long. So, as adults, that has coloured the way we feel most cherished.

- Remember, just as you would like to receive love in a certain way, others might like to receive love in a different way. Be open to expressing your love in the ways that they will enjoy the most, as long as it isn't beyond what you are happy to do.

No, no, no – how to know when to say no

We have had to learn to say no. It wasn't something that came naturally and, as young women, we feel very much that we were never guided or taught the importance of saying it. It's a skill which we really want to pass on to our audience, because taking control of your life – and not pandering to other people or trying to people-please – is vital if you are to reach your goals.

SO, HERE IS WHERE WE SAY NO:

- If something is not going to bring you joy or serve you in some way. Say no.

- If it's not going to benefit your life. Say no.

- If you think, I would have such a better day if I wasn't thinking about doing that thing that I said yes to. Turn it into a no.

- If you've got to think about it, you don't want to do it. So, say no.

- You're either all in, or you're out. It's either, hell yeah, I would die to do this. Or it's a no.

- Ideally, say no immediately. We try to be as assertive as possible, right from the get-go, when it comes to the no. Sometimes that is harder than at other times, and sometimes you feel you're in a situation where you can't say no. But as soon as you realise it isn't going to work for you, say no.

- It all comes back to you, and the fact that your purpose in life is not to please everyone you encounter. So, no, thank you.

- You can just cancel, it's usually not that deep. If it gets to the day of a plan, you have lost your chance to say no. So, follow through – no one likes a flake. (Unless there are valid, mitigating circumstances. Then feel free to say no.)

The Shape of a Healthy Relationship

Ideas for making your friend feel valued

MAKE SPECIAL PLANS. Something you can enjoy and share together. It can be very low key – watching TV or making a manifestation board. It doesn't have to be expensive. But you take control and organise and be thoughtful. Tell them to come over in their pjs, pizza is on the way. Make them feel that you want their company.

CHECK IN REGULARLY. Simply *tell* them that you're thinking of them. Make the effort with virtual communication as well. Be present in their life. Call, text, WhatsApp, FaceTime. Use all this

technology that is supposed to make our lives better, to make your friends feel loved. Just a text saying 'hope you're having a great week' can be enough.

SEND THEM SOMETHING IN THE POST. During lockdown we made a surprise gift box for each other. We set a budget and then ordered things to each other's house like a gift swap. Opening something you hadn't expected is such a wonderful feeling. If your budget is tight, send a letter or postcard. Just knowing someone has made the effort to go to the post office and probably queue for twenty-five minutes means a lot.

Networking for girls who hate it

IT'S ALWAYS BEST TO SEE NETWORKING FOR EXACTLY WHAT IT IS: WORK. While it would make the experience nicer to have a friend with you, if you know you're just going to speak to her all night, go alone.

SOMETIMES IT IS GOOD TO PUSH YOURSELF OUT OF YOUR COMFORT ZONE, TO GROW AND GET WHAT YOU WANT FROM A SITUATION. If we go to an event together, we can be insular. But when we go alone, we have to make more of an effort and chat to other people, and that is how connections are made.

MOST OF THE TIME WHEN YOU'RE THERE, IT'S FINE. It's getting yourself there and getting past your overthinking. And over-analysing every single step is the struggle. Just remember, so many people in the room will have been struggling with the same feelings in one way or another, however confident they might seem.

YOU CAN ALWAYS LEAVE IF YOU'RE NOT HAVING A GOOD TIME. You could be there for just twenty minutes. If you are really nervous, feel free to tell the people you are meeting or the event organiser that you already have another plan that night, so you always have an out.

IT'S NOT LIKE YOU HAVE THIS ONE-AND-ONLY CHANCE TO BLOW SOMEONE AWAY IN A NETWORKING SITUATION. You should just focus on leaving a good impression. Be pleasant and polite. Be a friendly face. You don't have to wow people or perform a skill to dazzle them. This is not *Britain's Got Talent*. Reduce your expectations of yourself and you will dial down the anxiety.

Difficult conversations 101

The feeling of dread before you have a tricky conversation can be all-consuming. But like everything, the more you do it, the easier you will find it to face up to intimidating exchanges. We have put together a little guide for how we now approach anything awkward, emotionally challenging or hurtful.

- **LAY IT ALL OUT.** Whittle it down to the key things that you want to get across and write them out as bullet points. If you struggle with remembering them, have them on your iPhone and feel free to refer to them if you get lost in your train of thought. Be organised and approach the situation almost professionally, as if it was a work presentation.

- **REHEARSE THE CONVERSATION WITH A CLOSE FRIEND.** Go over the key points several times and rehearse how you will say those lines. What you don't want to do is get there in the moment, panic and not say what you want to say.

- **WHAT IS THE PURPOSE?** When you are making your bullet points, think about what the purpose is behind this conversation. How do you want to feel after the conversation? What do you want answered after this conversation? Why are you doing this? What do you want to hear?

- **DON'T FAFF AROUND.** Be direct and assertive and say, I wanted to have this chat because A, B or C. I want to talk specifically about this because it made me feel like that, and I feel we need to talk it through.

- **LISTEN TO WHAT THE OTHER PERSON SAYS.** You have to be open to the conversation not going exactly as you planned. Sometimes in a situation you can one hundred per cent believe that you know you're in the right, and you've done nothing wrong, but then when you broach the subject you can be presented with an entirely different perspective which shifts your perception of events. You have to take a moment to reflect and accept responsibility where it's due. But don't let someone manipulate you.

- **SPEAK YOUR TRUTH.** The worst thing is building up to a conversation, finally having that conversation but then not saying what you wanted to say. Do not let that happen to you, *now* is the moment. Ideally in person, but FaceTime can be just as personable.

- **ADAPT AND BE FLEXIBLE.** If this conversation is with someone you are close to, remember that you know how they work and you know how you are going to get the best result from the conversation. There is a lot of advice out there that says you should always have difficult conversations in person, but perhaps a really good text would be better. Some people get very flustered in person; an email or a text gives the other person time to really read and digest what you've said, think about what they want to say and then respond with their points in a reasoned way.

- **ALLOW TIME AND SPACE FOR THEM TO CONSIDER WHAT YOU'VE SAID.** Sometimes doing it in person can be hard because it puts the other person on the spot. You've had all this time to prepare for this moment, and they're like, 'Sorry, what?' They might not know what to say. Give them time, tell them that you understand they may need some space to mull over the conversation. Don't demand an immediate answer, but set a time limit for you to revisit the issues raised.

The Shape of a Healthy Relationship

CHAPTER SEVEN

Breaking Out of Your Comfort Zone

In so many ways, we both had comfortable upbringings. Because we didn't go to uni and lived with our parents into our early twenties, we were able to work with each other from our family homes and we know how fortunate we were to have that opportunity. It was easy to create a solid comfort zone in Nottingham because we knew it inside and out, and we ended up both finding our own homes in Nottingham too. Of course, as we've spoken about, there were lots of challenges setting up our business because we didn't follow the traditional path after sixth form; however, in terms of taking really scary risks, we were really sheltered.

The flipside of that was that we both sometimes suffer from nerves whenever we have to do anything new or anything that involves a lot of change and that is something which we have both been confronting over the past year, because we are both so keen to gain more life experiences and understand our place in it. If you want things that require any kind of growth, be that gaining more experience, new skills or confidence, you are going to have to step outside of your comfort zone and that can be something you have to dig really deep to achieve. In this chapter we wanted to address some of your worries around growth and change as well as share some recent examples of where we have struggled. So much of dealing with stepping outside of your comfort zone is personal. Something that might seem super easy, almost casual for one person, could keep someone else awake at night for weeks. There are people out there who literally do not get intimidated about being the centre of attention, who can move countries without so much as a glance back and can start a new job without even planning their outfit for their first day. Obviously, there are lots of other people out there who have mental mountains to climb in order to even consider doing any of those things. It's easy to judge other people and say, they should just pull their socks up and get on with it, but it is just not that simple. You can desperately want to do something, but mentally and physically find yourself blocked from taking the steps you need to take to get there. That is something that we can really relate to, so we really wanted to discuss some of the ways in which we've been able to move things forward in terms of our goals, even as we've been consumed with worry.

Recently things came to a point where we started to feel like we've got to start practising what we preach. When a dilemma came in about moving country or quitting a job to start something new – or really doing anything daunting – we would always advise our audience to take the plunge. 'What's the worst that could happen?' we would say. But really, we hadn't been taking any big leaps of faith ourselves. So, when we reached a few crossroads in both our personal and professional lives, we decided it was time to be bold.

Dilemma One

I have older parents and recently they decided to retire to Spain and are selling our family home. I've been commuting for over an hour each way to my job in the city for the past two years and a lot of my friends have now moved away from our home town, so it feels like the natural time to move out myself. But even looking at listings for flat-shares makes me feel physically sick. I don't know what is wrong with me, I'm twenty-four now and it feels so lame to be so scared to do something that other people did years ago. How did you pluck up the courage to leave home?

S: Getting this flat in London was the best decision we have ever made, but it has taken us years to build up to it. We originally decided to rent our current flat because we were coming down to London literally every week. On the Monday we might have planned to have come down for two nights, but then our managers would ask us if we could extend a day or two because there was this meeting or that meeting on Thursday, and we'd suddenly find we were there for four days. Then it would be the weekend, so we thought we might as well stay. Before renting, we spent so long staying in hotels, which is obviously not sensible financially and it can feel so soulless. We were also spending so much time commuting that it was also hard to feel settled anywhere.

C: We were also basically living out of a suitcase. Permanently.

S: Because we both love our homes in Nottingham, which we have been so incredibly privileged to be able to buy, we wanted to live in them. But currently we are being pulled towards London on so many fronts that we had to be realistic with ourselves. Still, moving to a different city is a huge thing. Sometimes I can't believe it . . . we don't live in Nottingham any more! We've left our home town.

C: Two years ago, all anyone ever asked us was when we were going to move to London. But back then, we absolutely were not ready. I really was not attracted to the idea at all. Everything about it felt too much and we were so naïve that I think we would have felt very overwhelmed and out of our depth by such a big move. At that time, it would have been the wrong path to take.

But it just goes to show how much things can change, because now it has been such a smooth transition. In a weird way it doesn't feel dramatic or like a major change at all and I think that's because it happened over a long period of time. We first started spending a few nights here and there, then we got an Airbnb for a month, before finally making the decision to rent this apartment for a year.

S: Initially, I didn't process what moving to London really meant. We both were working on the idea that we would be going home all the time, and that this flat was simply a cost-effective place to stay for work. I really didn't think we were full-on relocating. When I went to Nottingham for that last weekend before we got the keys, my boyfriend was like, 'Do you want to pack up some stuff?' I said, 'Pack up? I'm not moving! This is just a temporary thing.' But moving full time is what has ended up happening.

C: This move was absolutely not on my agenda even a few months before we did it. I don't think either of us believed it was going to happen if I'm honest. I knew we would be in London a lot, but until it was actually happening, we were just focused on wheeling our suitcases across town.

S: I think, looking back, that I hadn't really acknowledged that moving to London was one of my aspirations. My parents have lived in Nottingham all their lives. My brother is in Nottingham, and he loves living there, so will probably be there for his whole life, which is amazing for him. The people that I'm closest to in the world have all stayed in Nottingham, so I suppose I just thought I'd be the same. But in retrospect, I always remember looking at my friends at work who went to uni and wishing that I had a reason to move cities too. I've always wanted that freedom and the idea of starting

The fear
of making
the wrong
decision
can stop
you from
doing
anything
at all.

afresh really excites me. I enjoyed living at home, but I was always looking forward to striking out on my own and having the chance to carve out my own life.

C: I didn't really feel that way when I was younger. I really do look up to people who move out of their family homes when they are sixteen or eighteen because I would have been shitting myself. I'd have been back home all the time or getting my mum to come over five days a week. I just wasn't ready at all because I think I was a very young eighteen and it took a little while longer for me to feel confident enough in myself away from my family.

S: See, I think I would have liked it. I think the thing is that when you miss that natural moment of moving after school for a job or uni, it can become even harder to find the courage to move away, which sounds like what you are experiencing. You become even more comfortable with what you know and the idea of starting all over again can feel so scary and out of reach – especially if you invest more and more in building a community around you where you are.

There were definitely hard moments after sixth form when everyone we knew started these new, exciting lives elsewhere on their own terms, while we were still in Nottingham, sleeping in our childhood rooms and letting our mums know what time we were going to be home in the evening.

C: It did feel like we hadn't moved forwards yet. While living at home is an incredible advantage for which I will always be grateful, it's not the most aspirational thing for a young adult.

S: Yeah, everyone we knew from school had left home when they were eighteen and were out the door, spread across the country. Whenever we met people at work – all these young kids from Manchester or Newcastle – they'd ask you where you were from, and you'd say, 'Here, actually.' Right.

C: I think the difficult thing when you're still living with your parents is watching other people do the opposite and having the best time. It just makes you feel like you're behind (another thing to make you feel behind!). All these other people building lives in new places and getting these experiences while we're in watching telly with our mums and dads.

S: Everyone else was growing up.

C: We got a taste of it by going to visit friends at uni or in their flats if they were working and we felt in awe of them. You can't help but wonder if your life is ever going to move on. But also, for me at least, there was a huge anxiety factor. I just felt like I didn't have the tools to form a circle of friends or rebuild my life somewhere new. I just didn't have that social confidence at all.

S: Since we have made the move, I've realised how much leaving your home town forces you to grow. You learn so much about the world and about yourself. If you don't have a huge number of ties or commitments to a particular city, starting somewhere new and taking that jump will benefit you more than you could ever imagine. It might not be in ways you had thought, but it will improve your life overall in ways you just would never expect. However daunted you might feel, if there is something that attracts you to trying it out, I would so recommend leaning on the people around you to support you through the transition. Perhaps your friends who are already in the city point you in the right direction in terms of areas to live, and they might even know of someone who is looking to share. Use your network to grease the wheels.

C: If you are umming and ahhing about making a similar move, I would try to see it this way: if you are just signing a year-long lease, just think that you're taking this year to develop as a person and see what happens. After a year, you either re-sign for another year, find a new place in the same city, or you move back home and say, you know what? – that wasn't the right decision for me. You can always try again somewhere else further down the line. The fear of making a wrong decision can feel so overwhelming that it can paralyse you from doing anything at all and you can end up missing out on so much joy because of that.

S: I think what we've learnt is that life, especially when you're young and you don't have major commitments, is about trial and error. If you don't give things a go, you'll never know. There is no right or wrong. Some people love their home town and absolutely want to stay there, there is no inkling in their mind that they'd like to try something else and that is so incredible for them. But if you do have that hunch that you might like to try living in a different place, I would so recommend throwing the dice, if you can make it work out financially.

C: Looking back at when we first came to London though . . . we were so clueless.

S: Yeah. We had absolutely no bearings and didn't know where we were – north, south, east or west – at any point. We had no idea what was good, which areas were which, where to go, what to do. Or what was safe and what wasn't. It was so disorientating, and I can so see why some people move and feel lonely, because building a whole new social circle really takes time.

C: But there are also positives to that. In Nottingham wherever we went, it felt like we knew everyone, and they knew us. It might be people we've never spoken to, but we recognised them because we'd seen them around.

S: We could probably quite easily trace them back and work out that they were so-and-so's cousin or friend. There would always be a link back to them. Wherever we go in London, on the other hand, no one looks familiar.

C: No running into ghosts from your past!

S: This sounds cringe, but it's also like we have had the opportunity to introduce ourselves in London instead of everyone thinking they already knew everything about us. A big fresh start with no drama. No one has any expectations of you or has heard any rumours. It's just a totally clean slate, which has been so amazing to experience.

C: We also love the variety of things to do and we are loving trying new places all the time. New experiences, new people, pushing ourselves out of our comfort zones and getting to know all the spots in our neighbourhood.

S: I personally feel like I have so much more purpose now. Whenever I go back to Nottingham, I'll love seeing my mum, dad and the dog. But then I'll get home and think, what am I going to do now then? My life has shifted south. It's not in Nottingham any more. It's happened over time, in a way that I didn't even really notice and I feel like maybe that has happened to you without you really even noticing it too. In London, I have work, friends, my boyfriend, my social life – our lives feel so full here.

Dilemma Two

My best friend and I have always talked about living together, but you hear so many horror stories that I've started to feel like it might ruin our friendship. How did you two manage to make the decision to move in together and have you regretted anything about the move so far?

S: So far so good! Hahahaha! No, being real, we're both really enjoying it. I remember when we moved into our own places in Nottingham, we were so excited, but I felt a slight pang of regret that I would never have the experience of living with a girlfriend or having a housemate. We'd not gone to uni and now we'd saved up to buy our own places, so that was that. I imagined if I were ever to live with someone, it would probably be a romantic thing. Now that life has moved in a direction we hadn't imagined, we have been unexpectedly offered this amazing chance to experience living with a best friend. Because we know it's not for ever, we are so grateful and appreciate it even more.

C: It has been really natural and easy.

S: It's been so chilled. I remember in the past when people would ask us when we were going to move in with each other and we would say '*Never.*' We always thought that as we were best friends, we worked together and we went out together all the time, we didn't need to live with each other as well. Perhaps that might not work for us? Like you, we worried that perhaps we'd be too on top of each other? But it's not felt like that at all.

C: I think it helps that we have heard literally thousands of housemate dilemmas over the years and what is so interesting is that so many of them follow the same themes. A successful flat-share needs a few elements. Firstly, you need to establish clear boundaries with the shared space. Secondly, you need space away from each other, and thirdly, it's important to prioritise really good quality time with each other. If Sophia has been away for the weekend, I will make sure that the communal space has been cleared and the kitchen is tidy before she gets back, because who wants to come back to someone else's mess? Sure, if I were living alone, I might leave the washing-up for the morning, but it's about being respectful of any shared space.

S: That is what most of the dilemmas we get focus on. 'I'm cleaning up after her', or 'She's taking advantage of me'. So, it's important to keep the mutual space tidy to sustain your housemate relationships.

C: There's also always the classic: 'Her boyfriend has been here for two weeks straight, and he's not left.' That is so not OK. Your boyfriend can come around, sure. But he can't be moving in or staying for extra-long periods of time. Is his name on the lease? Well, there's a reason for that. He can also do his own washing at home! No one needs to see his boxers drying on their washing rack. As for getting a bit of distance, some nights, I'll go and see my boyfriend or other friends and Soph will go and see her boyfriend. Sometimes Soph is alone, sometimes I'm alone. It's nice to have the flat to yourself from time to time, especially as we both enjoyed living alone in Nottingham.

But when we are home together, we make sure we do things together. We'll discuss what we're going to make for dinner, go and do the food shopping and cook and eat together without our phones or FaceTime or any other distractions. It's nice to have those moments together. We're used to being around each other all the time, doing work and having our friendship. So, moving in has just felt like an extension of that. It hasn't felt like stressful or difficult at all.

S: I feel like we have been really lucky with that. We know from the dilemmas that there is the chance that moving in together can cause challenges to even long-lasting friendships. It isn't a given that it'll work out. But we already knew each other's true colours to be fair. We've been on holidays where we've shared the tiniest little rooms with an even smaller bathroom. Like we *know* what each other is like.

C: With Sophia it wasn't like her dark side was going to suddenly come out. There wouldn't be a moment where I'd think, *Oh my God, I'm living with a devil.*

I think when you're considering who to live with because either a) you want a flatmate or b) it's not financially viable to live alone, the trick is to either live with someone whom you *really* know – like warts and all – or someone that you don't know at all, so things can be really clear and, I suppose, more contractual. I think choosing to live with someone you know a bit and is *kind of* a friend can really make things difficult if they turn out not to be the person you thought they were. There are so many grey areas when it's a friendship because you might feel uncomfortable saying certain things to someone who is supposedly a friend. This is often where the problem lies. You either need to be so close to someone that there is no issue with being honest, or have such little emotional attachment to them that it doesn't matter if they aren't your biggest fan.

S: If you can afford it, I also think you should never write off the idea of living on your own. Young women can be scared to live alone, and it's not really seen as the most fun option, but we both found it to be incredibly empowering. Obviously, if you're moving to London or to another very expensive city, it isn't going to be possible when you're just starting out. But if you can make it work it's worth it, even if it's a tiny cupboard of a studio flat all to yourself. If you don't have anyone you really want to live with, and it won't financially cripple you, I would so recommend considering it. To have a time in your life where you experience living alone is so beneficial. And just because you choose to live alone for a year doesn't mean you can't choose to move in with a flatmate the year after.

C: I can understand that people might think it would be a bit depressing or lonely or even sad to live alone. When you're young, you want to be social and the life and soul of the party. But you can still do both.

S: Overall, what I think is great is if you can become comfortable with the idea that you might live in lots of different environments in the moments between childhood and adulthood. After leaving home you might live alone, or with a partner or with friends, or all of the above. You might move cities, or you might move back home for stints depending on money and circumstances. You might buy somewhere, then go back to renting. You might do a gap year abroad, or you might get a job abroad. There just isn't necessarily that predictable 'live with mum, live in halls, live with friends, live with your boyfriend who becomes your husband' path these days and that can be really exciting. I also think that if you are desperate to move somewhere and take the next step, you shouldn't wait for ever to be able to afford the ideal living situation.

Young women can be scared to live alone but we both found it incredibly empowering.

If after months of saving you still can't afford to live alone in a new city, try to flat-share and let your new life take you in the direction you want to go. If you sign only a one-year lease, it won't be for ever.

C: Having a bad home situation can be the worst, because it's the one place that you want to be your sanctuary – your one little corner on the planet that is just for you. And if you don't feel happy or secure in it, that can have a really big impact on the rest of your life. So, it is worth thinking things through deeply before you throw yourself into anything – but not thinking for so long that you never end up making the move and moving your life forward along whichever path you want it to go.

S: For us, even though we never thought it would happen, it has been a great experience. Every day it feels like we're making memories that we never thought we'd have. I already know we will miss this flat. One day we will be driving past and think, *Good times! We used to live there!*

C: It just shows you how much life can change and that you can't predict or control everything. And also, when you manifest positive things, other amazing things will stem from them that are currently completely off your radar. You can't plan everything. It isn't like, T*his year I'm going to do X and the year after it's going to be Y.* You have to allow for organic developments and keep room for unexpected joys. Last year I didn't think this would happen, but here we are, so you have to bend with it.

Dilemma Three

Two of my best friends and I have always talked about sharing a house together, and now we're all working, we're about ready to move out. The only thing is that I've been with my boyfriend now for two years and I know he is massively keen for us to move in together sooner rather than later. I really love him and would love to live with him too, but also, I feel like this is my last chance to have this moment with my girlfriends and have this experience in my life. I know that my boyfriend will question why I would choose my friends instead of him, so I feel if I were to go down that road, I will need to work out how to phrase it right. Or perhaps I should just move in with him, because I do really think it's going to be a long-term thing? I wake up thinking one thing, then go to bed thinking something else, I just can't work out what I should do!

S: Our overarching, initial advice is to always try to pack in as much experience into your life as you can and always prioritise the things that you want. Which would point towards you taking this chance to live with your best friends.

C: Generally, unless you break up with your boyfriend, it would be unlikely that you would go back to living with a friend after moving in with him. If you have a wonderful, healthy relationship, you will hopefully stay together for many years and moving back out with a mate would inevitably cause doubts for your partner as well as all the logistical dramas. It's probably not going to happen.

S: Without sounding like a total cliché, you do have your whole life to live with a partner. The years that your oldest friends are all still single and looking to flat-share are, in contrast, limited. This time probably won't come around again, and you don't want to regret not having taken the chance to do something that you would love to do.

C: At the same time, I totally understand why you would want to live with your boyfriend. There was a moment in my life when I did too. There is always that pressure in the background of 'moving a relationship forward' and moving in with a guy is seen as the big step towards adulthood.

S: You're kind of told that your relationship should be progressing through these milestones and if it's not progressing through these milestones then it means it's not going in the right direction. 'We've been together for two years, so maybe we should live together, right?' If we choose not to, does that mean the relationship isn't going well? Or even going backwards?

C: Also, there's the fact that there is that pressure that you know your boyfriend wants to live with you and when you love someone you want to make them happy. You can feel like you have to say yes – especially if part of you wants to say yes anyway.

S: But what we would say is that there is just no rush.

C: If you see other friends moving in with their boyfriends, then just by default you feel like that is the standard of where you should be going and what you should be doing.

S: Don't get us wrong, when you get to that stage of moving in with your partner, that is so exciting. It should feel so positive and is something you really want to do and is absolutely celebrated. It's more that there is no rush to get there.

There is no price on the kinds of experiences you can have with your friends when you are young, and while I absolutely get that your boyfriend is probably dying to move in with you, you can't push down or minimise your true goals in life because it slows down someone else's plans. You just cannot live for someone else, you have to find the courage to make decisions on your own terms.

Perhaps think about saying, 'I'm so happy that you feel you want to live with me and I am so excited for when that time comes for us in the near future. But I feel just before we get there, for myself, I want to take this opportunity to live with my friends for a year or so.' Make it clear to him that it is because you see the two of you being together for the long term, meaning this is the only opportunity you will ever have to have this experience. It all goes back to the power of saying no and putting yourself first.

There is power in saying no and putting yourself first.

C: It's definitely worth putting the shoe on the other foot and thinking about how you would feel if the scenario was the other way around. You might feel like your partner wasn't taking you seriously if you really wanted to move in with him and he said he'd prefer to live with his friend. It could be very hurtful.

S: If the shoe were on the other foot and your boyfriend did move in with a friend instead of you, a lot would depend on his overall behaviour and how committed he makes you feel that he is. If he had a similar reasoning around seeking experience and reassured you that he was still very much on a track forward with you, that is one thing. But if he isn't offering you any suggestion that he does *actually* want to move in with you, the truth is, that perhaps he isn't taking you seriously as a longer-term partner. It's a delicate subject and absolutely needs to be handled with care and consideration because someone is inevitably going to feel deflated.

C: On the other side of the coin, if you were secretly leaning more towards moving in with your boyfriend and you were worried about hurting your friends' feelings, there's absolutely nothing wrong with choosing to live with your boyfriend, if that is what you really want. That is also a wonderful experience. You learn a lot about your relationship and yourself when you live with a partner. In a month your eyes could be opened.

S: When I was younger, I thought it was sensible to have a pretty long relationship with your partner before you decided to take the plunge and move in together. But now, I think the sooner, the better, because that's the only real way you're going to find out if a relationship is going to work in the long term or not. Moving in together offers a really amazing perspective on your relationship. Overall, I think the answer is that there is no real right or wrong here.

C: Whichever decision you make you will learn a lot and there are pros and cons to both. At the start when you move in with a boyfriend, it is very exciting, you feel very adult. It feels like a very grown-up thing. If your relationship were to work out, it is such a brilliant feeling. But make sure that it is right. If it's not, give it time – you are on your own clock, remember. Think how much you would love to live with your friends right now. Then imagine how you might feel in ten, fifteen years' time if you never do it. Regretting not taking an experience is the absolute worst.

Dilemma Four

Last week my boss suggested that I apply for a promotion on to the sales team within the company that I work for. I'm fine with my current job and I'd never really considered myself the 'sales' kind of person. It definitely makes my stomach flip over thinking about all the things that I wouldn't know how to do, but I'm also really flattered and know that it's a good opportunity for growth which probably won't come around again anytime soon. I'm just in two minds about what to do – stick with what I know and what I'm OK with, or try something which I could fail completely at.

S: Being flexible with unexpected opportunities as they come along is something that can completely change the course of your career. When you are young, saying yes to new things is generally always a good idea – unless it's a situation where someone is really taking advantage of you or treating you in an unacceptable way. For us, a really good, recent example of that was with our tour – that really wasn't something either of us would have put ourselves forward for and it certainly wasn't anything that was on either of our lists of ambitions or our manifestation boards. We were not *dying* to do it. But when we were offered the chance to host a series of *The Girls' Bathroom* live stage shows across the country – even though we were incredibly apprehensive – we could recognise that it was an incredible opportunity, so we decided to go for it.

C: Oh my gosh, we were so nervous. I can't actually describe how anxious we were. There were waterworks, telling our boyfriends we couldn't do it, the whole thing. The weekend before the first show, I couldn't see anyone at all because I just needed to gather myself and be calm. I remember that weekend was so daunting. There was this feeling that it was all on us to perform and make people laugh. But even though it scared us so much, we both knew this was one instance where we should say yes, not only because it would stretch us from a character point of view, but these kind of steps are what really make a career.

S: I think the most intimidating thing was that the shows weren't scripted at all.

Once you take the fear away and believe in yourself as a confident speaker, you open so many doors.

C: Yeah, it wasn't like I had this script to learn which would have been hard work, but once I'd memorised it, I would have been able to say to myself: I know my script, *I know what I'm saying, it's going to be great*. We didn't even know which dilemmas we would be answering on the day.

S: **It felt like we were totally winging it.**

C: And that was terrifying for me. You can get into this cycle in your mind where you start to think, I don't know what I'm going to say, and that can go into such a panic spiral. We hadn't even tried on our outfits, so I didn't even feel that sense of confidence in knowing what I was going to wear. There were so many little details that felt out of control.

S: **On the podcast we often say, 'Push yourself out of your comfort zone' and 'Do something that scares you.' Yeah, fuck it, 'YOLO!' It's so easy to sit there and say that, but actually doing those things is really tough. Even though the lead up to the tour was really challenging for us both, I felt unbelievably proud that we had taken our own advice to do something that made us feel scared shitless. And of *course*, it did really pay off in the end. We loved the experience so much more than we thought we would!**

C: We enjoyed ourselves so much. By the end of the tour, we were waltzing on to the stage as if it were our day job. Telling Michael McIntyre jokes, reusing these one-liners that we knew would make the crowd go wild. It was incredible seeing people have such a good time and it helped us gain so much confidence in ourselves. I feel like we can do anything now, it made us feel invincible. Honestly, now if I'm nervous in any social situation, I think, *Well, I've stood up on stage in front of 900 people up and down the country, so I can manage to meet my boyfriend's friends without spinning*. I think, *I've done that, so I can definitely do this*. Now I can go and meet new people and hold my own and not shit myself about it, which is a massive step forward for me.

Public speaking is such a major fear for so many people – engaging people and appearing confident is a real skill. Once you can take the fear away and believe in yourself as a confident speaker, you open so many doors. Whether it's at uni or in an office or a social setting, it's a skill worth having. To not be nervous to speak up and say something you want to say is something that so many of us struggle with. It feels so much easier to make yourself small and invisible. I would often think, *I'll just sit here and not say much and no one will notice me and I'll be fine and get through this.* That is OK, but if we're all going to grow into these young women who are sure of themselves and turn up for all the opportunities that come our way, you have to be able to say what you think in every environment.

S: Neither of us are naturally confident like that.

C: There are people out there who are fortunate enough to be born with those skills. We knew them at school. They were the entertainers of the class, the people who could say anything and get a laugh – we were never that. I'm funny in my small circle and funny with my family. But we were never these loud, gregarious performers. So, we were like, *How the fuck have we got ourselves into this situation where we're trying to make hundreds of people laugh like this?* But we did it!

S: That's why we would never have approached our managers to say, 'We want to do a tour.' It's hard enough having two people watching us while we're filming the podcast!

C: That's the thing. People always confuse our confidence onscreen or on our podcast with confidence performing in general. But with YouTube, when you're filming, you barely register it. You never think about the number of people that are going to watch it, because you would never be able to be anything close to natural if you thought like that. There is a sense of remove even though you are talking to an audience. For most of our working life, it's been just us two. When we were younger, we didn't have many friends and we got used to being in our own little space with the camera. In that context, it is really easy to get stuck in your routine and avoid any opportunities to expand your social skills and horizons.

S: The fear before the tour was real, but anything new is always daunting before you start. Then once you've done it you think, *I could do that again.* It's like anything – dates, exams, job interviews or new social environments – it's all practice and experience and it's never too late to gain new skills.

C: One of the funniest things about the tour was our boyfriends seeing us in work mode for the first time.

S: Our families and boyfriends came to see us at our last show and our boyfriends told us they were low-key mesmerised at the transformation.

C: To be fair to them, we had just spent a full weekend telling them that we couldn't do it. Mine kept telling me that I looked like I was about to cry. You have to remember that he knows me incredibly well and had seen that I'm not exactly the most self-confident person in most areas of my life. So, he was definitely thinking, *Fucking hell, are they going to be able to stand up there and do this?*

S: The same for me. On Sunday, I'm there at my boyfriend's, bawling, saying that I couldn't do it. Then Monday comes and it's like *helllllllo.*

C: 'Hello, London!' All confident in our Jimmy Choos.

S: They both said they were really scared for us.

C: And worried the whole time about what we were going to say next as we had really hammered the point home that we had no real idea what we were going to talk about beforehand. They just weren't sure if we were going to be able to carry the conversation for an hour and a half and to be fair, that was because we had told them we couldn't.

S: 'I didn't want to say, but before you went on, I was really panicking for you.'

C: 'I've got two girls here crying their eyes out. I don't think they're ready for it, they don't want to do it, what are we going to do?'

S: Anyway, we've decided that we're going to do it all again, so it can't have been that bad, could it! Hahahaha.

C: Taking the production values up a notch and going for it again.

S: However stressful it was before, seeing all those smiling faces and seeing our fans laugh was such an incredible life experience which I have so much gratitude for. Going into my DMs and reading messages from our audience saying that they had the best time and they wanted to relive it meant the world to us.

If you are being offered the opportunity to grow in a direction that at least somewhat interests you, you owe it to yourself and your future career to at least give it go, because the most likely result will be that you end up learning something amazing, even if you decide it's not for you in the long term. Could you possibly discuss a trial period with an option to step back into your old team if it doesn't work out? That would at least take some of the pressure off the decision. Either way, congratulations for being offered the chance in the first place – that is such an amazing vote of confidence which I'm sure you worked really hard for.

Dilemma Five

I am starting to lose confidence that I will ever get to where I dreamt of in my life. Last year, I won a government young entrepreneur's grant to help me launch a small market in my local area, but I'm finding that there are so many things going wrong the whole time, mostly because I have no real clue what I am doing. Some days I just feel like throwing the whole thing in and getting a normal job where I don't go home feeling like an absolute failure, but also, I know how great it could be if I could only iron out some of the bigger problems – it really would be my dream job. How do you go about your projects – do you have a project manager to organise all the logistical side of things?

C: This is every single business owner's story and probably a huge proportion of anyone in any field who is just starting out will feel the same too. When you are building something that is your actual dream, it can be so hard because it feels like there is so much at stake and the pressure around that can really get to you. But you have to keep the faith!

S: We have recently been feeling that kind of weight, because we have started to create a fashion collection and brand, something that has been a dream of ours for more than a decade. This was our biggest goal, our number-one target right from day one, when we were twelve or thirteen.

C: We have always had such a clear vision of what we want it to be.

S: And now we've moved to London and we're living together and it's all happening. And that is absolutely terrifying as well as, obviously, incredibly exciting.

C: We've been working more seriously for the last two years on putting the first collection out, and it was around tour time that we settled on the name. It has always been about finding the right time and the right people to help pull everything together. Obviously, we are complete beginners, and we have a lot to learn so we have had to build a team of people with all the expertise that we are currently lacking. It has been a huge process and we have met with so many people along that journey.

S: That's different investors, factories and creatives, and we have looked at all the different routes we could go down to make it a reality.

C: We also had to save a lot money for this because we have always wanted ownership of it. It's taken a couple of years to work out how the whole thing will run and now we have the best people on our side to fill the gaps in our experience.

S: Our role in the business is to guide the creative direction. The passion for us has always been creating the whole look and feel of the brand and the collections.

C: But we are so here to learn all aspects of the business from production to accounting too. One of our biggest ambitions with this brand is to understand the ins and outs of how a fashion business works.

S: We are so comfortable about saying that we don't know everything we need to know to do this on our own yet, and you should be too. If you run into a brick wall, it's time to start reaching out to find solutions that can take you to the next step. There's no point pretending that we're not really intimidated by the whole thing, because of course we are. It's like a whole new world to us and it feels like a huge leap as well as a massive risk. And then there's the bigger questions at the back of your mind: are people going to buy these things we're making? Because if they don't, our dream will just . . . be over. That's so scary because everything we have done to this day has been leading up to it.

C: There's a lot of pressure on it being completely perfect.

S: And we're really the ones putting the pressure on ourselves. We have been talking about this for years, so what's this collection going to look like then?

C: This first drop, what is it? What are the pieces, the prints? It has to be right. There's no 'that will do'. It has to be immaculate.

S: Generally, we don't like to rush things, so we have really taken our time. This time we call the shots, and we are in a position to say if it isn't good enough. If that holds things up, it holds things up. We are not going to sign off on anything that isn't exactly what we want.

C: So much goes into creating a product – from design through to sampling – it's just been such an experience.

S: But in, say, two years' time, we're going to be so much more confident and knowledgeable about every aspect of the business. The curve is steep, but we are starting something completely new and learning on the job. Imagine where you could be in two years of working towards your market.

C: We are keeping faith that everyone will like it, because we know that we are going to love it. And as long as our passion is in there and it's what we envisioned it to be, then naturally everyone who loves what we love, will like it too.

S: I think we're also realistic that not every business is this instant, massive success. Perhaps we don't end up getting to where we want to be for ten years. Or we might launch a new brand in our thirties or forties and that's where the story comes good. We just don't know what the next steps will look like, or timescales, and that again is really disconcerting. Perhaps we will look back and be like, remember when we were twenty-three and we had that brand? You just don't know what life is going to have in store for you.

But I know we will always think, we moved to London to follow our dreams and went on tour and created this book and started our brand. It was all kicking off at once. It's a nice little bubble of life that I know we will cherish, however hard some days may be.

C: All the things we have forced ourselves to do from launching our blog, to starting our channel, to the podcast, to dating, to moving home, to moving cities, to the tour, to launching the brand . . . those are all the steps that have transformed us from those sometimes insecure, nervous girls into two young women who are pretty confident. It doesn't just happen naturally for a lot of people. It is a step-by-step process of gaining experience and skills to grow and evolve over a period of years. Like you, we still have so far to go, but what we know for sure is that if something really scares you, but you can see the value in doing it, then that is the direction you need to go. If we did it – and honestly it still surprises us that we have – so can you!

The Ten Commandments: for housemates

1. Thou shalt not drink the last of the oat milk without replacing.

2. Thou shalt not slyly move your boyfriend into your room.

3. Unexpectedly bringing strangers into your shared space without asking is a no-no.

4. Thou shalt not use stress at work or uni as an excuse for sloppiness or messiness.

5. If thou can deal with it in five minutes, do not put it off (see paying the gas bill, loading the dishwasher, putting the hoover around).

6. Thou shalt not take your housemate for granted. Especially if you are friends.

7. Thou must never shave in the bath and not shower it down.

8. Thou shall continue to have your own life. No one likes a cling-along.

9. Thou shalt not disappear for days without letting your housemate know you're OK.

10. Thou shalt always be honest if your living plans change – never leave a housemate in the lurch with the lease.

Hate public speaking? Try these five tips

1. VISUALISE YOUR SUCCESS

So many of us spend time imagining screwing up or freezing on the spot when it comes to confronting our fears of public speaking. Instead, think of what it will feel like to nail the speech and for it to be a massive success. Set yourself up to win rather than fail.

2. DON'T BE SCARED OF SILENCE

In any kind of conversation there are moments of silence. When it's just you speaking, short silences while you recover your breath or work out the direction you are going in are totally natural. Do not freak out, instead use those moments to collect yourself and continue on to your next point.

3. PRACTICE MAKES PERFECT

For us, our tour was really a continuation of what we do on our podcast, so while we didn't know the actual material that we would be talking around, we were really sure of the set-up and the structure. If you aren't in the same position, the more comfortable you are with the kind of content you will be presenting the better. You can practise your speech from start to finish, film yourself, give the speech to people you live with – anything to make you feel more comfortable with the set-up or material.

4. ASK FOR SUPPORT

If you are really struggling, absolutely consider seeking help. If it's at uni, speak to your tutor to see if there are any programmes or support services that could help and if it's at work ask your boss about extra training. There are also professional coaches out there who can really help boost your confidence. While it may involve a financial outlay, speaking confidently is a skill that is worth its weight in gold. If you can't afford a formal class, look for public-speaking meet-ups or free online programmes that can help you. Asking for help isn't embarrassing at all.

5. REMEMBER: NEARLY EVERYONE GETS NERVOUS

It's estimated that nearly eight out of ten people are scared of public speaking and we're not really sure it's ever possible to totally get over the fear. In fact, we reckon it's probably better to be a bit on your toes, but it's about getting those nerves down to a level that you can manage and still get your point across. You are so not the only one that feels like this!

Our favourite things about moving cities

- Restaurants

- Independence – paying your own bills, doing your own laundry, cooking for yourself without relying on family or people you know to help

- More career opportunities

- Meeting new people with different life experiences

- FaceTime keeps you connected with your home town

- Your self-belief increases when you step outside of your comfort zone

- You can start with a clean slate and reinvent yourself as an adult

- You don't bump into people from your past whom you might prefer to avoid

You cannot live for someone else, you have to find the courage to make decisions on your own terms.

Quotes to inspire you

'Don't sit down and wait for the opportunities to come. Get up and make them.'

Madam C. J. Walker

'If you get tired, learn to rest, not to quit.'

Banksy

'There is always light. If only we're brave enough to see it. If only we're brave enough to be it.'

Amanda Gorman

'A flower does not think of competing with the flower next to it. It just blooms.'

Zen Shin

'The greatest mistake
you can make in life
is continually fearing
you will make one.'

Elbert Hubbard

'Today is your
opportunity
to build the
tomorrow
you want.'

Ken Poirot

Final Lil' Vote

Whenever we finish a project or achieve a goal we always try to take a little minute to reflect, before we skip on to the next thing – at least that's the theory, because sometimes life does take over. But we hope that as you finish this book you can find just a little space to have a think about everything we've covered. Perhaps it's some advice that has really resonated with you, or something practical that you've learnt and you really want to take forward into your life. It's so easy to gallop into the future without consolidating or considering what you've taken in, and that is something that we are working on too. We hope you can be present with this book. But if not, consider coming back to it when you do have the time and revisit the pages you've folded down, or the paragraphs you've highlighted. Make that date with a friend to work on your manifestation boards, carve out an evening to look into your cosmic profile, or simply flick back to something that made you laugh. (Hopefully there was something . . .!)

We so hope that this book has touched you and made you feel reassured, or at least less alone with some of the trials and tribulations that impact all of our lives. It's so easy from the outside to think that other girls are immune from these kinds of heartaches, feelings of shame or regret, and that other people all have wonderful, respectful relationships, full of love and devotion, with compatibility ratings through the roof. It's just not true – everyone has to weather the storms of relationship struggles and dilemmas. But that doesn't mean things can't be better in your relationships; that is a hundred per cent what we hope to work towards in our futures, and we hope we have inspired you to do the same.

Thank you so much for taking the time to listen to our stories and read through these pages. It absolutely means the world to us.

All our love

Soph and Cinz Xxx

Acknowledgements

Bringing this book to life has been a journey but we're so happy it's all come together and you are able to read and enjoy it. It's been an exciting, challenging and wonderful experience, and we'd like to take a moment here to thank everyone who helped make it a reality.

A massive thank you to the wonderful Katherine Ormerod, who helped us get our voices down on these pages and create a book that we know will help lots of women trying to find their way in life. You have been a dream to work with and we appreciate you.

Thank you to our lovely team at Margravine, who always believe in us and help us balance everything in life (which is not always easy!).

To our family, friends and loved ones who have always had our backs and support everything we do, we love you and are so lucky to have you.

Thank you to the designer Nikki Ellis and the illustrator Fabiola (@Ohkeidea), for making this book as beautiful on the inside as it is on the out.

A huge thank you to the Headline team: our editor, Katie, the PR and Marketing duo, Lucy and Alara, and all the other incredible people who have worked so hard to make this book become a reality.

And of course, thank you to our listeners, supporters and subscribers. For those who have been there from day one, and for those of you just now finding out about us from this book, we appreciate every single one of you and we hope The Girls' Bathroom book has brought you hope, inspiration and joy – you deserve it.